The Irish Episcopal Conference

WORK IS THE KEY

Towards an Economy That Needs Everyone

VERITAS

First published 1992 by
Veritas Publications
7-8 Lower Abbey Street
Dublin 1

Copyright © The Irish Episcopal Conference 1992

ISBN 1 85390 231 4

Cover design by Banahan McManus Ltd
Printed in the Republic of Ireland by
the Criterion Press Ltd, Dublin

CONTENTS

INTRODUCTION 5

PART ONE
The Context: Why We Are Writing Now 10
- (i) Poverty and Social Division 10
- (ii) Civic Culture and Public Morality 14
- (iii) Emigration and Our Self-Respect as a People 17
- (iv) The Need for Determination 20

PART TWO
The Teaching: The Contribution of Church Social Teaching 29
- (i) The Dignity of the Human Person 30
- (ii) The Dignity of Human Work 32
  - Work and Poverty 35
  - Work and Ownership 37
- (iii) Integral Human Development 38
  - Regulating Market Forces 42
  - The Virtue of Solidarity 43

PART THREE
The Application: Analyses and Responses to Date 52
- (i) Improving our Economic Stewardship 52
- (ii) Widening and Deepening a Consensus on Jobs 58
- (iii) Business Enterprise 59
- (iv) Empowering Communities and Regions 64
- (v) Job Creation and the Environment 67
- (vi) Jobs and Europe 68
- (vii) Justice While Unemployed 69
- (viii) Any Job is Not Better Than None 73

PART FOUR
The Spirituality: A Spirituality for the Challenge 87
- (i) The Spirituality of Work 89
- (ii) Respect for What is Public 89
- (iii) The Advance of the Kingdom of God 90

BIBLIOGRAPHY 94

INTRODUCTION

1. The unsatisfied hunger for jobs, with the unemployment and enforced emigration to which it gives rise, is the greatest single social issue confronting Ireland today. The current levels of unemployment, North and South – with their extraordinarily high incidence among some social groups and in some geographic areas – are causing suffering to an extent which is wholly unacceptable. More can be done to bring these levels down, and more must be done. We are aware of other terrible ills which scar the face of our society, especially poverty.[1] However, unemployment is exacerbating these ills and making them more difficult to resolve. Only when we improve our record in job creation shall we also make lasting progress in other areas of pressing social need. This fact, but primarily the sheer magnitude of our joblessness, has obliged us to adopt unemployment as the principal focus of this Pastoral Letter.

2. We recall with dismay that, when we wrote *The Work of Justice* in 1977,[2] the official unemployment counts in each part of Ireland, which we **then** thought constituted a grave challenge, were consistently below nine per cent. We write now when each part of Ireland is in danger of settling down to live with an unemployment count that can be **twice as high**. This is the crisis – that a grave evil has put down deep roots on our island and most of us are getting on with our lives, in fact acquiescing in what is the cause of deep suffering to a huge number of people in Ireland. While we recognise that factors outside Irish control can work against the creation of jobs here, sometimes very strongly, we regret nothing so much as a growing fatalism about the supposed inevitability of high unemployment and emigration for the rest of this decade.

3. The final preparation of this Pastoral took place at a time of gathering difficulties for the Maastricht route towards further European integration and of unprecedented turmoil in Europe's currency markets. While the crisis placed Irish monetary authorities and exporters in the frontline, it was fundamentally a chal-

lenge to the solidarity and maturity of our society as a whole. For example, all those working in the sheltered part of the economy were called to find ways of sharing the difficulties faced by the internationally trading sector for the sake of our whole society.[3] The vulnerability of our small economy to abrupt changes in international markets over which we have no control has been, and will be, repeatedly exposed. We believe that the ability of our society to cope speedily and equitably with such major dislocations will be increased if the values and priorities outlined in this document are widely adopted.

4. It is our conviction that work for everyone is today the single most embracing and ennobling project which can unite us, 'have' and 'have not', unionist and nationalist, man and woman, city dweller and country person, cleric and layperson. Ireland need not be the darkest unemployment spot on the map of the European Community. Since the early 1980s, unemployment has soared and, after each surge, more people have been left stranded in the ranks of the long-term unemployed. Only imagination, energy and solidarity will bring unemployment down by the end of the decade. Our confidence that such a project is attainable is reinforced by the depth of the desire for work that we have met in individuals, families and local communities. They are unambiguous in stating what they most want in order to meet their needs: 'a decent job!' Unemployed people long to earn their income and to do so in a way that respects their freedom and the dignity of their work. In their eyes, even a guaranteed adequate income from social security would be only a half-way house. Even well-funded, efficient and courteous social welfare systems, therefore, would not discharge society's obligations towards its members who are unemployed, nor enable them to discharge their obligations towards themselves. High unemployment is not something to be 'lived with'; it ought to be banished from our island.

5. What follows will betray a sympathy for certain approaches. Some people may legitimately prefer others. We would not, even if we could, propose a blueprint for job creation and income redis-

tribution for our competence is religious and, therefore, ethical and human, not economic.[4] Our aim is to enter into a dialogue with all Irish people about the deeper meaning of the extraordinarily high unemployment levels we are tolerating so as to strengthen their desire to help bring it to an end, to deepen their awareness of how that can be achieved, and to mobilise a public consensus on making employment the top priority.

6. It is true that none of us individually, nor any single group to which we belong (trade union, employers' organisation, professional association, voluntary or community group, etc.), can **solve** the problem of unemployment and its attendant emigration. However, we believe it is also true that the problem **will not be solved without us**. No-one should expect that the mobilisation of resources, imagination and energy that is needed to tackle unemployment will be achieved without them. This Pastoral invites each person, each group, to reflect on how they can contribute something further to the cause of effective solidarity with the great number of our people seeking jobs.

7. We write also, and in a particular way, for those who seek to follow Jesus Christ more closely in our divided society of today. To our own faithful, and to all other Christians whose reflections and suggestions we welcome as enriching our own, we say in this Letter that the struggle to make Irish society, North and South, more responsive to the work needs of its population is a potential place for encounter with Christ. There you will experience something of the reality of sin and of how insidiously it diminishes the humanity of both sinner and sinned against; there you will learn some of the cost of discipleship today and of the meaning of the preferential option for the poor; there you will perceive the wholly unexpected presence of the Holy Spirit; there you will become part of a Church that is a servant of the Kingdom of God; there you will find another concrete means of expressing that universal love which is the hallmark of the Christian.

8. In the preparation of this Pastoral, we have received generous help from women and men engaged at every level in the economy, North and South – unemployed people, managers of large international companies, trade unionists, economists, financiers and others. We have been actively assisted by our own Episcopal Commissions, by theologians, and other advisors. The Council for Social Welfare took the important step of issuing a discussion document, *Unemployment, Jobs and the 1990s*, and varied, but always valued, responses to it were received from individuals, groups and associations throughout Ireland. To everyone who has helped us we are deeply grateful.

9. We have decided to include references to various studies on Ireland's socio-economic affairs in the text of this Pastoral. This is not because we, as bishops, were able to verify all the analyses and conclusions of these studies but because we believe it is important that we try to situate our concern for values and principles, as much as we can, in the context of the actual policies being debated, introduced or modified today. The references will help people to see that the struggle to live by the values and principles of the Gospel is, in fact, taking place daily around us; we are not starting from scratch. They will also help study groups to assimilate in a critical manner what our Pastoral Letter is talking about.

10. We earnestly hope that the process of consultation and dialogue which has marked the preparation of this Pastoral will intensify and deepen after its publication. We do not see publication as an end in itself but as contributing to the clarification of the root causes of our high unemployment and emigration, and to the fostering of the solidarity needed to combat them.

REFERENCES

1   A Pastoral which set out to address comprehensively social injustice in Ireland today would, perforce, have to decry, among other things, political violence, crime, homelessness, abuse of alcohol, drug addiction, violence against women, child abuse, discrimination against the travelling people, overcrowded prisons.

2   *The Work of Justice: Irish Bishops' Pastoral,* Dublin: Veritas, Publications 1977.

         We returned to some of the major themes of *The Work of Justice* in:

         Christian Faith in a Time of Economic Depression, A Statement from the Irish Episcopal Conference at its General Meeting, 15 June 1983; and

         Emigration: A Pastoral Letter from the Bishops of the West of Ireland, Sunday 15 March 1987.

3   For an analysis of the links between the sheltered and the exposed sectors of the Irish economy, see The Council for Social Welfare, *Unemployment, Jobs and the 1990s*, Dublin: The Council for Social Welfare, 1989, paras.54-58, pp.25-27, especially para.57.

4   'We see ourselves as **facilitators** of a process which we hope will lead to constructive changes in the lives of our peoples. We are not experts in any of the relevant areas; we have not got executive power; we are not trying to tell others their business; quite simply we are using our **collective voice** to highlight a growing social problem....' (Bishop John Kirby, Bishop of Clonfert, Closing Remarks to 'Developing the West Together', Seminar sponsored by the Bishops of the West of Ireland, Galway, 4-5 November 1991, p.1)

PART ONE

The Context: Why We Are Writing Now

11. If we do not courageously face together the high unemployment which is so deeply rooted in our society at present, and in danger of being accepted by the majority who are at work, it will recoil on all of us. The quality of life for a large number of people will remain abysmal and our society will become even more sharply divided; our already fragile civic culture and commitment to the common good will weaken further; and emigration will undermine our self-respect as a people and reduce our country's influence in world affairs.

(i) Poverty and Social Division

12. Society, in both parts of Ireland, seems to have surprised itself by its ability to survive high and protracted unemployment. In the North, there is a **notional** acceptance that lack of satisfying work (and, consequently, of a meaningful adult role for many young people) is increasing the attractiveness of participation in paramilitary organisations. However, because the region is, in fact, surviving its high level of political violence, there is a sense that 'settling down' with endemic, high unemployment is relatively easy by comparison. In the South, it was once thought that an unemployment count that passed the 100,000 mark would trigger the downfall of the government. Now, because inflation is low, the balance of payments sound and the national debt under relative control, it appears that an unemployment count approaching 300,000 can be 'lived with'. In both parts of Ireland, many among the majority who have jobs believe that the situation of most unemployed people is made tolerable by what they think are reasonably good social security payments and/or earnings from the black economy.

13. The reality, which none of us finds easy to face, is that we have been unable to provide between one-fifth and one-quarter of our

people who want a job on this island with the opportunity to participate in the mainstream of economic life here. They must take their chances as immigrants in other societies or remain at home and risk living featureless, dead-end lives entirely dependent on our social welfare systems. It needs to be said, again and again, that the most damaging cost of unemployment today is being borne, not by the taxpayer, but by those individuals, families and communities who have had it thrust upon them. Some people naively reassure themselves that things could be worse because no unemployed person is actually starving. Others point out that if unemployed people can smoke and watch videos, clearly they can be enduring no great hardship. The sad truth is that, behind relatively ordinary hall doors, many unemployed people are battling to keep their health, self-esteem, relationships and family lives intact in the face of quite exceptional difficulties.

14. These difficulties include:
- the sense of rejection that comes from the experience of repeated, unsuccessful job hunting. The self-confidence of the unemployed person is worn down by failure after failure to get a job. A feeling of inadequacy can become deeply rooted. A father can feel humiliated at the poor role model he is providing for his children still at school, young people can feel they have failed their parents, a woman can feel she was never meant to relate to a world outside her home. Unemployment strikes deeply at a person's feeling of self-worth.

- the constant and often impossible battle of wits involved in 'making ends meet' when the weekly income is insufficient for the bare necessities. Poverty research in the Republic has demonstrated conclusively that long-lasting unemployment during the 1980s threw more and more people into poverty, and that many of the heads to be counted are those of the children of unemployed people.[1] While the standard of living of poor households in Ireland does not involve destitution as in a Third World situation, it is relentlessly restrictive. Not only is diet dependent on cheap filler foods but there is no money to replace furniture, decorate the home, purchase normal household durable goods, provide adequate clothing for adult family members or enjoy family outings.[2] Long-term unemployment squeezes variety and security out of living standards.[3]

- the dreariness of a monochrome existence, unbroken by opportunities to make choices in life and denied all chances of planning for a brighter future. A job for most people is a powerful support to structuring their daily lives, for linking them with the wider world and giving them a sense that their lives are going somewhere. Unemployed people, on the contrary, struggle with boredom. The personal ordering of their lives becomes difficult, a difficulty compounded by the arbitrary way they can be summoned to attend interviews by welfare and training authorities. It is hard for unemployed people in their twenties to feel positive about the future when their c.v. is already such as to make it unlikely that they will ever be offered a decent job. Unemployment cuts people off from a future worth working for.[4]

- the desperate plunge into emigration although a person has insufficient qualifications and contacts to make a proper new beginning in another society. There is substantial evidence, for example, that a significant number of Irish emigrants to Britain continue to be unemployed, impoverished and vulnerable young people. Already in Britain are our emigrants of earlier decades, for some of whom becoming unemployed or growing old in a country not their own is proving a lonely and harsh experience. Sadly, people of Irish origin are disproportionately present in Britain's psychiatric institutions and among its homeless.[5] Even in the case of better qualified emigrants, it can happen that being Irish makes it difficult for them to find the social and occupational status that they could otherwise have expected. Involuntary emigration too often results in marginalisation or occupational underperformance in another land.[6]

15. We could speak of yet further difficulties caused by unemployment. Our concern here, however, is to help bring home to every person that the poverty on this island, although it is primarily

what sociologists term 'relative' poverty rather than 'absolute' poverty, is, nevertheless, deeply disturbing and damaging. It is extensive no matter what actual measure is used.[7]

16. 'Relative' poverty is the fruit of an unacceptable degree of inequality. It occurs where people's income is so far below the average in their society that they are unable to take part in, and do, what is regarded as normal. We are told that nearly 6 out of 10 households, where the head is unemployed, must live on an income that is **less than half** the average income in the Republic today.[8] Yet, we must remember that the members of these families window-shop in the same streets, watch the same TV channels and tune in to the same radio stations as the rest of the population. They cannot escape what is presented as evidence of success, freedom, popularity, and the false associations which modern advertising seeks to build between particular products and deeper human needs. We often hear people who have reasonably good incomes comment that unemployed families should budget better. Wasteful expenditure, however, is far more conspicuous among the well-to-do than among people who are poor. In fact, it is, sadly, sometimes the case that money spent by unemployed people on cigarettes or cable-TV brings them greater emotional satisfaction and, thus, better all-round human well-being than if the same money were used to improve their diet.

17. If all this is not enough to make every person on this island detest unemployment, those unconvinced should consider how the unemployment of so many others is negatively affecting their own lives. It is depressing national output far below what it might otherwise be; it is diminishing tax revenues while raising public expenditure; it is leading more people into crime and anti-social behaviour than would otherwise happen; it is feeding substance abuse and homelessness. A society in which so many of its people are marginalised through unemployment is a society which ends up increasingly on the defensive. The growing emphasis on security in the design of middle-class housing suburbs and apartment blocks is a sad witness to this fact.

18. Faced with such worrying evidence that we are in the process of intensifying an unhealthy dualism in our economy and society, we value greatly the work of those Church and other bodies who do so much to keep the reality and the challenge of this before our conscience as a people. In focusing this Pastoral on joblessness, however, we are drawing attention to the principal factor that has been fueling social inequality and eroding the will and the means for dealing with it effectively. Church social teaching points out the direction policies must take if our totally unacceptable degree of poverty is to be overcome: '...**human work is *a key*, probably *the essential key*, to the whole social question...**' (*Laborem Exercens*, n. 3, emphasis added).[9]

(ii) Civic Culture and Public Morality

19. In addition to being a blight on the quality of life of a huge number of people, we see our present levels of unemployment as simultaneously reflecting and nurturing a weak civic culture. In the context of this Pastoral we take civic culture to mean people's sense of identity with, and responsibility for, each other as citizens and their regard for what is public. If civic culture were strong, for example, it would mean a disposition to pay tax rather than avoid it because individuals would trust that all were being treated equitably and that public revenue was being efficiently and wisely used to build and protect the common good in a transparent way. Regrettably, this does not describe society in either part of Ireland today. Rather, an attitude is prevalent which regards any tax payment which can be avoided, and every social welfare transfer or public payment which can be brought in, as 'fair game'. There seems to be broad tolerance of behaviour which consists in 'doing what you can get away with'. The resulting legacy of tax evasion,[10] of substantial investment in tax avoidance, of strong lobbying for grants or for special treatment in the tax code, of lax moral standards in asserting entitlement to social welfare payments or in making out invoices to public authorities, constitutes a grave moral malaise.

20. Building a strong civic culture requires that we practise high standards of public morality. Public morality applies to every aspect of people's relationship with one another in society. It refers, therefore, not just to how we approach our tax responsibilities, but, among other things, to our use of everything that is publicly funded (social welfare receipts, business grants, health and education, emergency services, as well as tax allowances, etc.); to the pricing of our services in commercial transactions; to the prompt payment of debts especially by those with the greatest economic 'muscle'; to our respect for the law and for legal procedures; to our truthfulness and sense of responsibility on the media; to our participation in associations, trade unions or other public bodies; and to so much more.

21. People in positions of authority have a responsibility to lead the way in setting high standards of public morality. Sadly, however, there is growing cynicism in Ireland towards authority, in politics, business, public administration, the trade unions and in the Churches. This cynicism, we believe, is a greater danger to the health of our democracies than many care to accept. It is perhaps understandable to find it among unemployed people where it is fed by their sense of being blamed for their unemployment and let down by the educational system. The offer of inconsequential training courses or short-term work is regarded as a pale substitute for a real job. They feel aggrieved at not being consulted. The poor amenities and social problems of some public housing areas can make the very address of unemployed residents an obstacle in their search for work. It is our sad experience that, even where the gift of baptism has been widely received, the people and communities in question often feel alienated from our Church too, as well as from public authorities and the political process.

22. What makes cynicism and alienation even more of a threat to our civic culture, however, is that it is also widespread among the job-holding majority. The difficulty of reaching agreement on the political future of Northern Ireland; business scandals interwoven

with the political culture of the Irish Republic; the experience, in both parts of Ireland, that people's local and parliamentary representatives are also in the dark about what is decided by cabinet ministers and senior civil servants (for example, in negotiations within the European Community) – these are some important factors which have acted to deepen disillusionment with the democratic process in the recent past.

23. For some time there has been evidence that our civic culture in Ireland compares unfavourably with that in those other small European countries whose employment performances we would like to emulate[11] and that the reason is historical in an important degree. So, for example, the nationalist community in Northern Ireland is continuously tempted to regard the civic and public fabric of its life as alien and biased against it. In the Republic, a long history of colonisation left people with a weak sense of responsibility for public processes but, for the first decades of Independence, a strong religious obedience helped make good this lack. As an exaggerated sense of individual autonomy and an over-absorption in material things have worked to lessen people's religious convictions, so only weak roots have been left to their public morality and the near-absence of a civic culture has become exposed.[12] Society has little to fall back on. We see the renewal and strengthening of these religious roots as a central element in the building of a strong civic culture.

24. The current weakness of Irish civic culture makes it much more difficult to mount an effective campaign for jobs. A mobilisation of our society to improve on job creation, however, will spur growth and development in our civic culture. This is because a renewed appreciation of the nature of human work as an essentially collaborative and social activity – '...*work with others* and *work for others*...' (*Centesimus Annus*, n.31),[13] – will help inject new solidarity into our social fabric.[14]

(iii) Emigration and Our Self-Respect as a People

25. Unemployment threatens not just social cohesion and civic culture on this island but leads to a level of emigration that undermines our integrity as a people. Every society produces members who choose to build their lives in other lands. No one, however, who has stood in Irish airports or ferry terminals at the end of a Christmas holiday period will be fooled into thinking that the emigration which characterises this island is normal, a simple sign that our youth experience the attractions of Europe and the rest of the world. The pain of family separations, the anger of young people returning to the status of migrant worker after having experienced once again, for a brief period, the attractions of being in their own country, the gloom that descends on streets and neighbourhoods in place of the bustle and vitality generated by the brief reappearance of the young, all give a further insight into the pernicious effects of joblessness on our society.

26. Involvement in the process of growth towards greater unity in Europe is, generally, a positive development in Irish life, even one that is capable of occasioning a fresh perspective on the political conflict in Northern Ireland. Today, in fact, the Republic finds itself with a responsibility and power, beyond what its economic weight or population would suggest, in an organisation whose future development is critical to the whole of Europe and to relationships between the rich and poor worlds. However, as the Single Market, to which we committed ourselves in 1987, takes effect, the willingness of Irish people to remain jobless or in poor quality jobs on this island will diminish even more. The first to leave are, and will continue to be, the young and the better qualified whose flexibility and skills are essential to a more rapid development of our economy. Our failure to provide satisfying work on this island, therefore, is adding a push factor to the already considerable centralising forces being stirred up by the Single Market and serving to pull companies, capital and people into an economic heartland beyond our shores.

27. Dubbing this involuntary emigration 'labour mobility' or 'internal migration' serves only to camouflage a serious social reality or, what is worse, to suggest that the seriousness of the situation is exaggerated. If the large, net outflow of our youth resumes, it will only increase the prospect that, eventually, the larger European states will accord the position of the Irish Republic similar weight to that of a region in the Community (equal to, for example, Sicily, Galicia or Northern Ireland) and the Irish Government's influence on the Council of Ministers of an enlarged Community will be minimal. Only regions within larger national entities concur – and, even then, not always willingly – with the indefinite and large **net** movement of their youth to other territories for work.[15]

28. Some people said that a basic soundness in the Irish economy during 1991 and 1992 was concealed by alarmingly high unemployment levels. They pointed out that the surge in unemployment was the spillover effect of an exceptionally long-lasting recession in Britain which made many previous emigrants return as they opted to be unemployed in their own country rather than abroad. The rise in unemployment, they went on, did not reflect otherwise sound 'economic fundamentals' such as the low inflation rate, balance of payments surpluses, overall competitiveness of companies, the downward trend in the Debt/GNP ratio, etc. The advice given, accordingly, was to 'sit tight' and wait until economic recovery in Britain enabled emigration to pick up once again. A perspective based on Catholic social teaching, however, points out that nothing is more fundamental to the sound functioning of an economy than its ability to provide satisfying jobs (see Part Two). Such a perspective positively valued the surge in unemployment in 1991 and 1992 in so far as net emigration, for a while at least, was ended and we faced, finally, the **one** underlying problem. The true magnitude of the demand for work looked our society in the face and at last a sense of urgency emerged about the need to deal with it. It would be tragic if a resumption of substantial net emigration were to allow deep attitudinal, structural and policy changes to be avoided.

29. The Bishops of the West of Ireland have been able to facilitate many people in the west in finding their voice together to shout 'stop!' to further emigration. They speak from a part of Ireland where the population has fallen by 24 per cent since 1926, from rural districts where as many as 2 out of 3 young people emigrated in the late 1980s, from areas where, for many, not emigrating means working long hours on small farms to wrest an income that is scant reward for the work put in and utterly inadequate to ensure a decent livelihood for a family – in short, from a countryside where forests are fast replacing people and their homes. They know the difference between 'labour mobility' and the death-throes of a way of life. The exodus of their youth has seriously impaired the quality of life in rural areas so that now the viability of local businesses, schools and parishes is threatened. Theirs is not a voice against the east nor against city dwellers but a voice registering a willingness to work, and to work together, for the integral development of that part of Ireland where they live. In each of the other provinces, not excepting Leinster, there are rural communities whose experience is mirroring that of the west because of the haemorrhage of their youth. The initiative, therefore, of the western region gives them heart and is powerfully in the interests of all of us on this island and, indeed, throughout the European Community. Rural communities have a right to expect the system to work with them and support them. A genuine listening to the western voice will require a willingness to assist in strengthening local and regional structures through which responsibility and resources can be as close as possible to the people on whose response everything ultimately depends.[16]

30. It is true that a significant objective of the Single Market is the free movement of people to different employments. This is a valuable way in which people gain experience, skills are shared and shortages of workers for particular tasks are overcome. The present high unemployment in Ireland makes it not just realistic but wise to seek opportunities for immediate work for our people elsewhere in the European Community. But each person who gets a job overseas should be an additional reason for intensifying,

rather than slackening, our efforts to develop the economies on this island. Recent emigrants should remain, not just in our hearts but, for example, on the lists of our training and placement authorities. Each time a person emigrates involuntarily, we should look forward to the day when our economy and our society will be able to offer them a satisfying job here.

31. Our observance, each year, of Emigrants' Sunday is one way in which we try to keep alive in our hearts that those who have involuntarily left this country to find a job remain, nevertheless, part of us. 'The migrant ... cannot be disassociated from the people to whom he or she belongs....' In every migrant the nation in which that person has roots '...is to be respected, since it is a community of people, joined by various ties, by a language and especially a culture, which constitutes the horizon of life and integral progress.'[17] It is important, in particular, that we assume our responsibilities for those of our emigrants who find themselves vulnerable to financial or social exploitation. We salute those agencies and individuals who, on all our behalf, strive to support them.[18] The fact is that involuntary emigration in search of work '...is the loss of *a subject of work*, whose efforts of mind and body could contribute to the common good of (his or her own) country, but these efforts, this contribution, are instead offered to another society which in a sense has less right to them than the person's country of origin' (*Laborem Exercens*, n.23).

(iv) The Need for Determination

32. Pope John Paul II describes unemployment as '...in all cases an evil...' (*Laborem Exercens*, n.18). It is so because it eats away at the self-respect and self-reliance of individuals, families, communities and of this island as a whole. It is an enormous affront to the dignity of the human person and to the unity and sanctity of family life in Ireland today. How then can we live so complacently with it? Only an intense and practical indignation, undiluted by rationalisation, by selfishness, or by the kind of excuses which sound weak and unac-

ceptable to unemployed people themselves, can generate the kind of resolve that the present situation demands. This indignation is not a transient emotion nor a self-righteous anger but a real, continuing, concrete determination to overcome the evil.

33. It is not easy for unemployed people to become aware of the root causes of their joblessness, much less to express indignation about them. They first need to guard against self-doubt which their failure in the labour market feeds, against apathy which is the fruit of boredom, against stress and ill-health brought about by joblessness and its attendant financial insecurity, and against a general lowering of their expectations produced by the pessimism in the country concerning job creation. Yet everyone in Ireland needs to hear their voice. How else can society know about the ravages of unemployment? How can it come to realise that what is said about unemployed people can often be an unwitting rationalisation, or the product of selfish indifference or of simple ignorance? Clearly, those who support the efforts of unemployed people to find a collective voice are performing a valuable service to the whole of society.

34. It is difficult too for people who have a job to feel the necessary indignation. Many people in this situation also struggle financially, not admittedly to repay loans at small grocery stores but for needs that have become essential to their job and way of life such as a housing mortgage and keeping a car on the road. They experience helplessness and frustration as unavoidable expenses suddenly increase to jeopardise plans they had made and commitments they had entered into. The high taxation that many people pay on their earnings makes them vulnerable to seductive voices suggesting that the income transferred to unemployed people (rather than that used to service the national debt, or to fund public sector pay increases or the large number of tax reliefs) is the real culprit. The day-to-day lives of people who are long-term unemployed are unknown to them. This is partly the result of the unfortunate way in which housing policy has interacted with

unemployment to produce some areas of our cities and towns where people are almost totally dependent on public housing and transport and live with local unemployment rates of 60 per cent or higher, while other areas have unemployment rates in single figures and a way of life dominated by home and car ownership. Those whose own lives and families have not been scarred by unemployment need, above all, to listen to their unemployed brothers and sisters. No-one can teach us so much about the importance of having a job in Ireland today as those who have been years without one.

35. The words spoken by Pope John Paul II in Brasil can be applied to Ireland. They express what we believe is needed in order to redress social division, strengthen public morality and civic culture, and ensure our self-respect as a people.

> 'How much suffering, how much worry and misery unemployment causes! For this reason the first and fundamental concern of one and all, rulers, politicians, trade union leaders and owners of enterprises, must be this: to give work to everyone. To expect the problems to be solved as the more or less automatic result of an economic order and development, of whatever kind, in which employment appears as a secondary consequence, is not realistic and therefore is not admissible. Economic theory and practice should have the courage to consider employment and its modern possibilities as a central element in their aims.'[19]

REFERENCES

1   See T. Callan, B. Nolan and B.J. Whelan, D.F. Hannan with S. Creighton, *Poverty, Income and Welfare in Ireland*, Dublin: The Economic and Social Research Institute, 1989, (General Research Series, Paper No.146), pp.101-110, and Brian Nolan and Brian Farrell, *Child Poverty in Ireland*, Dublin: Combat Poverty Agency, 1990, n.6.3, pp.57-60; Chapter 7, pp.66-74.

2   Jo Murphy-Lawless, *The Adequacy of Income and Family Expenditure*, Dublin: Combat Poverty Agency, 1992.

3   For research on Irish poverty see, in addition to 1 and 2 above:

Northern Ireland Voluntary Trust, *A Qualitative Study of Life in the Disadvantaged Areas of Belfast*, Belfast: Northern Ireland Voluntary Trust, 1991;

Combat Poverty Agency, *Pictures of Poverty: Twelve Accounts of Life on Low Income*, Dublin: Combat Poverty Agency, 1989;

Eileen Evason, Les Allamby and Roberta Woods, *The Deserving and the Undeserving Poor*, Derry: Child Poverty Action Group (Northern Ireland), 1990;

Pauline Lee and Michael Gibney, *Patterns of Food and Nutrient Intake in a Suburb of Dublin with Chronically High Unemployment*, Dublin: Combat Poverty Agency, 1988.

4   To understand just what life in Ireland today while unemployed can be like, read:

Tallaght Centre for the Unemployed, *Life on the Dole*, Dublin: Tallaght Centre for the Unemployed, 1991;

Northern Ireland Voluntary Trust, op. cit., Part I, pp. 15-35;

Chapter 1, 'A Tale of Two Cities', in Catholic Social Service Conference, *Dublin: Hard Facts, Future Hopes*, Dublin: Catholic Social Service Conference, 1988;

Chapter 1, 'The Effects of Unemployment', in The Council for Social Welfare, *Unemployment, Jobs and the 1990s*, op. cit.

Christopher T. Whelan and Damian F. Hannan, Sean Creighton, *Unemployment, Poverty and Psychological Distress*, Dublin: The Economic and Social Research Institute, 1991 (General Research Series, Paper No. 150);

Chapters 5-10 in Eileen Evason, *On the Edge: A Study of Poverty and Long-term Unemployment in Northern Ireland*, London: Child Poverty Action Group, 1985 (Poverty Pamphlet 69).

5   Briefings from Innisfree Housing Association, London, 1992.

Liam Greenslade, 'White Skins: White Masks, Psychological Distress Amongst the Irish in Britain', in Patrick O'Sullivan (ed.), *The Irish in the New Communities*, Leicester: Leicester University Press, 1992.

6   On recent emigration see:

National Economic and Social Council, *The Economic and Social Implications of Emigration*, Dublin: National Economic and Social Council, 1991 (Report No.90);

The Irish Episcopal Commission for Emigrants, *Emigrant Survey 1991/1992*, Dublin: The Irish Episcopal Commission for Emigrants, 1992;

The Irish Episcopal Commission for Emigrants and The Catechetical Association of Ireland, *Far Away Hills: Christian Perspectives on Emigration*, A Manual for Teachers and Group Leaders, Dublin: The Irish Episcopal Commission for Emigrants, 1990;

Emigrant Advice, *Annual Report 1991*, Dublin: Emigrant Advice;

The Information Needs of Emigrants, Report of a Seminar Jointly Organised by The Action Group for Irish Youth (London), Emigrant Advice Unit (Belfast), Emigrant Advice (Dublin) and the National Youth Council of Ireland, Dublin, 9 December 1991;

Frank P. Forsythe and Vani K. Borooah, 'The Nature of Migration Between Northern Ireland and Great Britain: A Preliminary Analysis Based on the Labour Force Surveys, 1986-88', *The Economic and Social Review*, Vol.23, No.2, January 1992;

Geoffrey Randall, *Over Here: Young Irish Migrants in London*, London: Action Group for Irish Youth, 1991;

Maggie Pearson, Moss Madden and Liam Greenslade, *Generations of an Invisible Minority: The Health and Well-Being of the Irish in Britain*, Liverpool: Institute of Irish Studies, University of Liverpool, 1991 (Occasional Papers in Irish Studies, No.2);

Liam Greenslade, Maggie Pearson and Moss Madden, *Irish Migrants in Britain: Socio-Economic and Demographic Conditions*, Liverpool: Institute of Irish Studies, University of Liverpool, 1991 (Occasional Papers in Irish Studies, No.3).

7   See Callan *et al*, op. cit. and Carey Oppenheim, *Poverty: The Facts*, London: Child Poverty Action Group, 1990.

8   We are told, for instance, that when the average home in the Republic ran a 17.5 per cent risk of falling into poverty (1987), homes headed by an unemployed person ran a 60 per cent risk. (See Callan *et al*, Table 7.11, p.104.)

9   Pope John Paul II, *Laborem Exercens* (On Human Work), 14 September 1981, London: Catholic Truth Society.

10   The extent of the abuse of the tax system in the Republic revealed by the Amnesty granted in 1988 is one confirmation of this. It yielded almost £500m. An Amnesty granted in 1991 to those with arrears of Capital Acquisitions Tax (CAT) payments yielded £13m – the target having been £5m. The reduction in the tax clearance threshold for State contracts and grants in the same year yielded over £18m in outstanding tax. (See The Revenue Commissioners, *Annual Report 1991*, Dublin: Stationery Office, July 1992.)

11   For example, Austria, Denmark, the Netherlands, the Scandinavian countries, Switzerland.

12   The weakness of civic culture in Ireland is noted by, among others, J.J. Lee, in *Politics and Society: Ireland, 1912-1985*, Cambridge: Cambridge University Press, 1989, and in 'Society and Culture' in Frank Litton (ed.), *Unequal Achievement: The Irish Experience 1957-1982*, Dublin: Institute of Public Administration, 1982.

An ESRI study of young people's experience of their schooling found a 'disturbing level' of pupil and school indifference to civic-political education. It commented: 'As our society becomes more complex, and it becomes more difficult and complicated to devise and negotiate economic and political solutions to our very serious problems, it is disturbing to find that the main institution that could increase the knowledge and competencies of our young people in their civic and public roles places such little emphasis on this objective' (D.F. Hannan and S. Shorthall, *The Quality of Their Education: School Leavers' Views of Educational Objectives and Outcomes*, Dublin: The Economic and Social Research Institute, 1991, General Research Series, Paper No.153, p.6).

13   Pope John Paul II, *Centesimus Annus (The Hundredth Anniversary)*, 1 May 1991, London: Catholic Truth Society.

14 'The culture which our age awaits will be marked by the full recognition of the dignity of human work...' (Congregation for the Doctrine of the Faith, *Libertatis Conscientia (Instruction on Christian Freedom and Liberation)*, 22 March 1986, London: Catholic Truth Society, n.82).

15 'It cannot be regarded as a success for a region that its principal export is its young people, for it is on these young people – their skills and their talents – that a region's success ultimately depends' (Belinda Pyke, Member of Cabinet of EC Commissioner for Regional Policies, Address to 'Developing the West Together', Seminar sponsored by the Bishops of the West of Ireland, Galway, 4-5 November 1991, p.13).

16 See Papers of 'Developing the West Together' Seminar;

Bishop Thomas A. Finnegan, 'Developing the West Together', *The Furrow*, Vol.43, No.4, April 1992;

John Healy, *No One Shouted Stop*, Achill: The House of Healy, 1988 (first published as *The Death of An Irish Town*, by Mercier Press, Cork, 1968);

John Healy, *Nineteen Acres*, Achill: The House of Healy, 1987 (first published by Kenny's Bookshop, Galway, 1978).

17 'Migration and the Unity of the Human Family', Papal Message for World Migration Day (issued 10 September 1991), *Catholic International*, Vol.2, No.19, 1-14 November 1991, p.904.

18 For example, The Irish Episcopal Commission for Emigrants; The Irish Commission for Prisoners Overseas; Emigrant Advice; the many Irish chaplains working overseas and the Irish Centres in different countries.

19   Pope John Paul II, Address to Workers at São Paulo, 3 July 1980. (See 'Collaborators of God in the Work of Creation', *L'Osservatore Romano*, Weekly Edition, 21 July 1980, p.5.)

PART TWO

The Teaching: The Contribution of Church Social Teaching

36. In the face of complex questions concerning what is economically and politically feasible if we are to reduce the level of unemployment in Ireland today, we are aware that, as bishops, we have no particular expertise in economics or business affairs. Yet we earnestly wish to make that contribution which is appropriate to us.

37. We speak as the pastors of a Church which has been, in God's Providence, entrusted with a marvellous message about the grandeur and struggle of what it is to be a human being. We fervently desire that this message, which God shared with all humanity through His Son, Jesus, should be a real source of Good News and liberation to all on this island who are anguished by persistent, high unemployment.

38. Ours is also a Church which, down through the centuries but particularly since the onset of the industrial revolution, has developed a body of **social teaching** whose guiding principle is a correct view of each human person's unique value (*Centesimus Annus*, n.11). We are, therefore, building on a long tradition when we seek to relate Gospel truths to the complex reality of industrial society and the global economy today. With this Letter we seek to encourage more Irish people to become familiar with this social teaching and to discover **for themselves** its application to the circumstances of our economy today.[1] There are, meanwhile, some basic orientations and guidelines which it is our duty as teachers of the Catholic faith to enunciate clearly.

39. Our contribution, then, to the resolution of unemployment is primarily to help clarify and strengthen the **human purpose** and necessary **ethical framework** for economic activity in Ireland today. Much of the debate about unemployment inevitably explores what is attainable within existing political and economic

constraints. Deeper values in the cultures on our island, however, may be capable of influencing what is feasible in policy terms because their strength or weakness helps to determine what will, or will not, generate electoral defeat and what will, or will not, occasion serious economic resistance (such as tax evasion, capital flight, industrial unrest, etc.). We want our contribution to help strengthen some fundamental values whose present weakness we see as contributing to the intractability of the current unemployment problem. In this way, we hope this Pastoral will help to widen the boundaries of what is politically possible and, therefore, of domestic economic policies.

(i) The Dignity of the Human Person

40. The first of the fundamental values which we seek to elaborate on is one which we know we share with practically every Irish person today – but, sadly, in the light of the continuing violence in Northern Ireland, not with everyone – the incalculable worth of each human being.[2] We are grateful that Catholics and many other people throughout the world today witness, in multiple ways, to the dignity of the human person.[3] This is not accidental but integral to witnessing to the Gospel.

41. Concern for human dignity has frequently led us to make clear our abhorrence of political murder and abortion. In this Pastoral, we wish to make it clear that we see unemployment also as a denial of the dignity of the human person, made in God's image. We repeat, with great sadness, as pastors in this country, that unemployment '...in all cases is an evil...' (*Laborem Exercens*, n.18).

42. Jesus in the Gospels is full of indignation at whatever hems in or limits the potential of people's lives.[4] So, too, the followers of Jesus today are filled with a 'deep amazement' at human worth and dignity (*Redemptor Hominis*, n.10)[5] and accept that, in the final analysis, their entry into Heaven hinges on how well or how badly they treat other people in this life (Mt 25:31ff).

43. For Catholics, and all Christians, the foundation of this awe at human life is religious. We see every single human being as made in God's image and know that the human being '...is the only creature on earth which God willed for itself...' (*Gaudium et Spes*, n.24).[6] Not just at the creation of the first Adam but in the case of every individual we understand that the creative activity of God Himself is the indestructible foundation of a new human existence (Gn 2:7). A human being invites our reverence because, in her or his presence, we are also in the presence of God's image.

44. The authors of the Bible texts came to this profound insight under the inspiration of the Holy Spirit even though the human being then seemed puny relative to the forces and immensity of the natural world. Today, we are called to witness to the same religious insight when the sheer numbers of the human race and the concentration of the prodigious powers of science, technology and economic forces in the hands of a few threaten, once again, to make the individual appear insignificant.

45. This reverence for the human person is the foundation of the Christian's preferential option for the poor. As in the time of Jesus Himself, so it has continued in the societies of every subsequent generation of Christians down to our own, that the human dignity of people who are poor is insulted and defiled by the conditions of life which are forced upon them in their poverty. An integral part of Christian witness in every society is to seek out and relate as sisters or brothers to those people whom a process of impoverishment has thrust to the margins. We are aware of, and grateful for, the many ways in which this witness is being given in Ireland today. There are individuals and organisations sharing a deep sensitivity to the need for solidarity among, and with, people who are poor.

46. The insight of the Bible that the human being, alone of all creatures, is made 'in the image of God' (Gn 1:27) has stirred the hearts of every generation of believers. For example, it is clear to the Christian that the God in whose image we are made is not a

solitary person but a unique family whose mutual relationships and self-giving establish the substance and the pattern for all authentic human living. This means that no person is an island; everyone is called to intimacy and to the give-and-take of relationships with others.

(ii) The Dignity of Human Work

47. In this Pastoral, we would like to highlight another aspect of what the Church has understood in this biblical text. The God in whose image we are made is depicted as a **working God**. With the beautiful story of the God whose labour over six days created the universe and then gave the human race full responsibility and stewardship for the earth (Gn 1:26-28), inviting the first human being to be a co-worker at the very dawn of creation (Gn 2:19), the Holy Spirit, through the biblical authors, has revealed to us what human experience confirms – that work is a 'fundamental dimension' of humanity's existence on earth (*Laborem Exercens*, n.4).

48. A second fundamental value to which we seek to draw the attention of everyone, therefore, is the value of human work. In the Christian understanding, human work is any and every activity that is, at the one time, both building up the individual as a human person and contributing to others, including the wider society of which she or he is a part. Pope John Paul II has given us a long and searching reflection on work in *Laborem Exercens*. There, he points out that work is 'a universal calling' (n.9), that through it a person not only transforms nature but also achieves fulfilment as a human being and '...in a sense becomes more of a human being' (n.9). People, he goes on, 'must work' because their own humanity requires work in order to be maintained and developed. They must work out of regard for others, especially their own families but also out of regard for the society to which they belong, the country of which they are citizens, and the whole human family of which they are members: 'All this constitutes the moral obligation of work...' (n.16).[7]

49. It is sometimes important to distinguish between 'work' and a 'job'. This is because not all human work is organised in the form of a job as, for example, the commitment of the homeminder, of those caring for infirm or aged relatives, of the student, or of the vowed religious. It is also true that not every job measures up to the requirements of human work as, for instance, when low pay or oppressive conditions demean and injure the person of the worker, or when the nature of the job constitutes a direct attack on the dignity of others (for example, filming pornography, being a torturer, manufacturing chemical weapons). However, we wish to state clearly that, in our view, the fundamental moral imperative of honouring every person's need and right to work translates, in the Ireland of today, into the imperative of creating more jobs as an essential means to that end. We have heard no convincing argument nor seen any evidence that there is a sound alternative to job creation if we are to respect the vocation to work and, consequently, the human dignity of that huge number of our people who are unemployed.

50. Society can only be deeply troubled when it reflects on how the relationship between work and the dignity of the human person is 'radical and vital' (*Libertatis Conscientia*, n.83).[8] In the Christian understanding of the human being, it is **part of being human** to want, and need, to work. Work is a process of basic self-expression and self-assertion by a person without which her or his very humanity remains only partially developed. This, in turn, gives all human work a claim on our attention and respect, for to put a low value on someone's work is to put a low value on that person.

51. We believe that in humble and, sometimes, heroic ways many people on this island are giving witness to the dignity of human work despite pressures to the contrary.

- It happens when people refuse to be dragged down by the low standards that have become accepted by others in their company or union but, in lonely integrity, keep honesty, application and respect for others as hallmarks of their personal work.

- It happens when people fight to improve the rates of pay and conditions attached to particular jobs, including those pertaining to special labour market schemes. They are insisting that such 'jobs' measure up to the requirements of human work.

- It happens when people demand that work which unemployed people would undertake, or may already be engaged in doing voluntarily (sports training of youth, community development activities, etc.), should be put on a paid basis. They are insisting that resources be assigned to work which society needs to have done so that this work can be organised into proper jobs.

- It happens when people accord respect and esteem to what others are doing even though no wage or salary is being paid for it, or is ever likely to be – work in the home, the work of study, much of the work of members of religious orders, etc.

- It happens when people oppose extreme differences in rates of pay because they are aware that, when one person is cleaning the corridor and another is engaging in multi-million pound transactions by phone, although there are different risks and responsibilities, in each case a human being is using her or his gifts to respond to God's invitation to make the world a more fit place for all His children.

In all such instances we celebrate and give thanks for the presence of the Spirit of Jesus, Jesus who said: 'My Father goes on working, and so do I' (Jn 5:17).

52. This perspective on work, this answer to the question 'why work?', constitutes a noble and a challenging task facing all who have a role in preparing young people for adult life. Parents, teachers, instructors and lecturers will readily appreciate how important it is to convey to young people that they have a contribution to make, whatever it is, that their contribution is needed and will be valued, and that it is worthwhile preparing themselves for making it. We have heard, and understood only too well, their

pain and frustration that so many young people still emerge from formal schooling more aware of what they lack than of what they have, and that a very large number hear Irish society say 'there is no room for you' by offering only a choice between unemployment, dead-end jobs or emigration.

53. It is, of course, not just in our personal attitudes and behaviour that reverence for the dignity of human work must be expressed but in the **collective** obligations and restraints that we undertake as a society. Church social teaching draws our attention to some key consequences for other areas of our society of this understanding of work: it vitally affects the way we seek to eliminate poverty, and the way we seek to regulate the ownership of productive property.

Work and Poverty

54. The Church has been aware, particularly since the time of *Rerum Novarum*, Pope Leo XIII's great encyclical *On the Condition of Workers* (1891), of the intimate link between work and poverty. When a low value is put on people's capacity for work poverty flourishes and claims new victims. Pope Leo committed the Church to the defence of working people and their right, always and everywhere, to a just wage. In defiance of the dominant economic thought of his time, he pointed out that working people and employers were in such unequal positions of strength that the fact a worker agreed to a wage did not thereby make it a just one: '...a requirement of natural justice higher and older than any bargain voluntarily struck...' demanded that the wage be sufficient to support the worker (*Rerum Novarum*, n.34).[9]

55. This thought has been continued and enriched to our present day. The Church still sees much poverty as the fruit of the violation of the dignity of human work, '...either because the opportunities for human work are limited as a result of the scourge of unemployment, or because a low value is put on work and the rights that flow from it, especially the right to a just wage and to

the personal security of the worker and his or her family' (*Laborem Exercens*, n.8).[10] What justice requires is simple and clear: '...in every case, a just wage is the concrete means of *verifying the justice* of the whole socioeconomic system...' (*Laborem Exercens*, n.19).

56. Employment, in the perspective of Church social teaching, should, therefore, be the first bulwark against poverty. When, for whatever reasons, society cannot provide employment, a fundamental principle of Church social teaching must be honoured which recalls that 'God gave the earth to the whole human race for the sustenance of all its members, without excluding or favouring anyone' (*Centesimus Annus*, n.31). Church social teaching calls this the principle of 'the universal destination of the earth's goods'. It follows that an unemployed person is entitled to an income which allows him or her to live with dignity and to its sensitive and courteous administration. However, justly remunerated employment remains the norm towards which Church social teaching points us:

> It is '... necessary above all to abandon a mentality in which the poor – as individuals and as peoples – are considered a burden, as irksome intruders trying to consume what others have produced. The poor ask for the right to share in enjoying material goods **and to make use of their capacity for work**, thus creating a world that is more just and prosperous for all' (*Centesimus Annus*, n.28, emphasis added).

57. We have heard, again and again, the desire of people who are poor not only to live better through having more, but also to be accorded the dignity of earning. They seek to **participate** in bringing about an improvement in their standard of living and the building-up of a better country. This makes all the more tragic the instances in which an unemployed person has to turn down an offer of employment because the wage being offered is simply too low, and/or because social protection (for example, public health

care, help with rent for housing) is withdrawn so quickly that his or her standard of living takes an abrupt fall.[11] It is to add insult to injury to interpret this need of unemployed people to protect their already precarious living standards as evidence of 'work shyness' or that they want 'money for nothing'. Disincentives arising from interactions between social welfare, taxation and low pay should, indeed, be dealt with, but any action taken must not worsen the situation of unemployed people.

Work and Ownership

58. The Church in its social teaching has also considered the rights and responsibilities of ownership, and the balance that has to be struck between respect for the economic initiative of the individual and respect for the right to work of everyone.

59. It has arrived at a clear conviction that ownership of property carries '...a social mortgage... in order that goods may serve the general purpose that God gave them.'[12] It also understands that, in a modern industrial society, the 'property' which is socially accountable includes, in an important way, people's know-how, technology and skills. There was a time when the decisive factor of production was the land; later it became capital. Today the decisive factor is more and more the capabilities of the human person, that is '...human knowledge, especially scientific knowledge, (the person's) capacity for interrelated and compact organisation, as well as (the) ability to perceive the needs of others and to satisfy them' (*Centesimus Annus*, n.32). In Ireland today, a moral obligation to facilitate job creation falls on a broad spectrum of ownership. For example, the Church, in its social teaching, is clear that, morally, 'the only legitimate title' to the possession of the means of production '...is *that they should serve labour...*' (*Laborem Exercens*, n.14); that such ownership '...morally justifies itself in the creation, at the proper time and in the proper way, of opportunities for work and human growth for all' (*Centesimus Annus*, n.43).[13]

60. It will escape no-one that this perspective on ownership is deeply lacking in many aspects of Irish life. While people in their hunger for a decent job have been literally wasting away, urban property sites have been left unused for long periods as their owners watched their capital value increase; large financial sums have played the money markets on behalf of companies whose business is something totally different; people with considerable business skills and expertise have grown wealthy by following avenues which led to virtually no job creation; companies have folded and jobs been lost because the owners of the assets preferred to liquidate them and enjoy the financial receipts rather than undertake the hard work of developing their resources in the interests of the common good; financial sums have sat, at home or overseas, bringing their holders small but safe returns while small and medium enterprises, whose expansion would bring wide social benefits, have been stunted or have failed because they could not obtain capital.

(iii) Integral Human Development

61. The same Christian tradition out of which we make these observations on the dignity of human work and the responsibilities of ownership, has come to describe the wider historical process, in which every person's capacity for work and every owner's property finds its appropriate use as 'integral human development'. Such development is '...an imperative which obliges *each and every* man and woman, as well as societies and nations ... a duty of all towards all...' (Sollicitudo Rei Socialis, n.32).[14] No person, therefore, least of all a Christian, should neglect to make her or his contribution to the '...personal and collective effort to raise up the human condition and to overcome the obstacles which are continually arising along the way' (*Sollicitudo Rei Socialis*, n.31). The third fundamental value which we seek to highlight, therefore, is integral human development.

62. The Second Vatican Council reflected on the deeper meaning of the power given the human family by its growing mastery of

science, technology and the techniques of production. *Gaudium et Spes*, its *Pastoral Constitution on The Church in the Modern World*, made it quite clear that economic activity, as with all human activity, benefits the human family, and does not prove ultimately harmful to it, only when it is carried out 'within the limits of morality' (n.64). When it respects those limits, 'all the elements making for development' – such as '...technical progress ... a spirit of initiative, an eagerness to create and expand enterprises, the adaptation of methods of production, and the strenuous efforts of all who engage in production...' can together '...unfold the Creator's work ... and contribute to the realisation in history of the divine plan' (n.64; n.34).

63. All of us, because of where we live and the times in which we live, are called to assume our individual role in what is today a vast, collective undertaking, namely, '...authentic development, a development which is for each and all the transition from less human conditions to those which are more human' (*Populorum Progressio*, n.20).[15]

64. The more resolutely Church social teaching has asked people to become involved in this socio-economic undertaking, the more it has sought to clarify the moral boundaries which economic activity must respect and to identify just what constitutes 'more human' living conditions. For example, it has insisted that economic growth must respect and promote human rights, the cultural and religious sensitivities of each people, and the integrity and variety of creation.[16] In Ireland, today, for a great number of people, 'more human conditions' begin with having a job.

65. What we have already said[17] about the vital bond between work and authentic human living has made it clear that, on the level of the individual, living better for a human being **includes working better** and cannot be attained at the cost of ceasing to work or of working in a way that offends human dignity. In keeping with this, integral human development, at the level of people and society, has to feature the widest possible **participation** of

people in economic life.[18] Economic growth merely measures increases in the level of economic activity. In its turn, it must be measured by ethical yardsticks of what is good for individuals and for society as a whole. If the process of growth, for example, disemploys people on an enduring basis, it has become a tyrant and not a servant.

> 'The obligation to earn one's bread by the sweat of one's brow also presumes the right to do so. A society in which this right is systematically denied, in which economic policies do not allow workers to reach satisfactory levels of employment, cannot be justified from an ethical point of view, nor can that society attain social peace' (*Centesimus Annus*, n.43).

66. A greater commitment to job creation is not fulfilled by simply calling for more and different types of State intervention. That is important,[19] but the State, on its own, cannot solve the current unemployment crisis. The problem is much deeper. While it is true that Ireland is failing the ethical test of integral human development most prominently because of unemployment, this is partly because our island has begun to share in a general moral malaise affecting all 'Western' industrialised societies. This malaise is making it increasingly difficult for any of them to redirect economic activity in ways that the integral good of their people requires.

67. The problem arises from the way in which success at economic growth becomes addictive to those who have already benefited from it.[20] Growing up in any society should entail learning from several sources (family, religion, school, movements and associations etc.) about what it is to be a human being and a member of one's people at a given time in history. Only a culturally-mediated understanding of who one is, and of how the history of one's people is unfolding, properly assigns economic activity its place and confers on it its meaning. A constant theme in Catholic social teaching is the primacy of the non-economic aspects of culture and the role of the economic dimension as a **means** towards larger

purposes. In the West, however, the inverse appears, sadly, to be the case. It is economic activity which increasingly gives purpose to individuals and to society. This is an absurd inversion of what makes for full human living.

68. It needs to be said again and again that society is more than an economy. The prodigious success of science and technology in flooding the market-place with new products and services can mesmerise people. A better 'standard of living' becomes understood in a one-dimensional way as purely the ability to enjoy increased purchasing power. But, as the concept of integral human development makes clear, the quality of human living is vitally dependent on things which the market cannot produce but which, alas, it can significantly erode, such as family and community relationships, social peace, a clean environment, cultural and spiritual attainments and – of particular importance in Ireland's case – the opportunity to work.[21]

69. The poverty of a culture which makes economic growth the fundamental purpose of society, rather than subordinating that growth to a wider hierarchy of values, is nowhere more evident than when it denies all intrinsic value to work. When people choose what to do, and measure the worth of what they do, solely from the perspective of what brings in more money, they are degrading their own humanity and contributing to the debasement of human work. In occupation after occupation today, an obsession with money and a narrow concept of efficiency are in danger of diminishing the personal care and inter-personal relationships that should imbue people's work.

70. It is our role as bishops to ensure that the Christian faith challenges this 'error of economism' – the mentality which considers human labour '...solely according to its economic purpose' (*Laborem Exercens*, n.13).

> 'If economic life is absolutised, if the production and consumption of goods become the centre of social life and soci-

ety's only value ... the reason is to be found not so much in the economic system itself as in the fact that the entire socio-cultural system, by ignoring the ethical and religious dimension, has been weakened...' (*Centesimus Annus*, n.39).

71. If society and culture do not accept and accommodate the multiple social manifestations of the hunger for God in the human heart, they will become impoverished. This happened in the former Communist countries (*Centesimus Annus*, n.24) but it is a central question also for the West. A culture that turns its back on religious faith will lose the ability and the will to give human direction to economic growth, technological advance, business enterprise and market forces.

Regulating Market Forces

72. An important way in which culture proves stronger than economics is through the willingness of society to regulate market forces responsibly. Church social teaching makes it very clear that we are not faced with a choice between the command economies that proved so intolerable in Eastern Europe and the abject worship of the market. Uncontrolled and blind market forces favour the powerful and neglect the weak. The free market is an instrument to be respected and used but never given the role of final arbiter of how society is shaped, be it in either part of Ireland or in the European Community as a whole.[22]

73. When we in Ireland argue the case for receipts from the European Community's Structural Funds – and even for automatic fiscal transfers at a future date to compensate for the centralising forces that are being strengthened by the creation of the Single Market – we are implying that, at home too, we will willingly carry out whatever institutional innovations or increased transfers are necessary to keep individuals, social groups and regions from being excluded by market forces from full participation in the life of our country.

74. While the State has to exercise constant vigilance and show great resolution in harnessing market forces to the cause of integral human development, the individual can never morally invoke 'market realities' to justify harsh or indifferent conduct towards others. Market forces as such have no morality, but the people who take financial decisions and who make economic choices within the market system do have moral responsibilities. Their decisions and their choices are moral acts, governed by the moral law and by conscience.[23]

The Virtue of Solidarity

75. As Church social teaching has reflected on the challenge which an increasing mastery of economic production presents the human family, it has stressed that the integral human development which is so badly needed will be impossible without a 'simultaneous development' (*Populorium Progressio*, n.43) of the virtue of solidarity. Solidarity is a responsible and loving acceptance by a person of the fact of human interdependence on a global scale today, of the fact that one's own life and the lives of countless others whom one will never come to know personally are intertwined for good and for ill.

'(Solidarity)…is a *firm and persevering determination* to commit oneself to the *common good*; that is to say to the good of all and of each individual because we are *all* really responsible for *all*. …(It) helps us to see the "other"…as our "neighbour", a "helper" (cf. Gn 2:18-20), to be made a sharer, on a par with ourselves, in the banquet of life to which all are equally invited by God' (*Sollicitudo Rei Socialis*, n.38; n.39).

76. Solidarity acknowledges the indivisibility of genuine development. One social class, one region of a country, one country in the international economy, cannot consider itself 'developed' if that situation has been achieved at someone else's expense. This virtue should be the hallmark of the Christian today, and of every person

who has begun to appreciate how the 'common good' is that of the human family as a whole. People animated by this virtue in Ireland will seek job creation and economic development in a way that is truly supportive of how the European Community and the industrialised world in general should be assisting the world's weakest economies, especially those of Africa but also those in Central and Eastern Europe. There can be no question of aid going to the Southern hemisphere or to the societies being reconstructed in the former Communist bloc being classed as somehow 'lost' to Ireland. Even less can trade concessions be resisted as 'not in our interest'. We need their successful economic development if we are to be fully ourselves, just as they need ours.

77. Within Ireland, the greatest test of solidarity is, of course, whether the majority on this island who hold jobs wield effectively the power they have to change a situation in which unemployment is being forced upon so many others. They do this, first of all, through the quality and integrity of their work. An economy which is frequently disrupted by industrial disputes, or whose goods and services are of inferior quality or more expensive than those of other industrial societies, is passing up opportunities to involve more people in jobs.

78. In the second place, employers and workers have to accept that what each takes out of the enterprises they jointly constitute can, and sometimes does, affect the ability of the overall economy to expand. If all adopt as their reference point the fees, perks, salaries and wages which richer economies are able to pay, it is probable that they will selfishly corner for themselves much of the benefit to the Irish economy of participating in the Single Market. This would be grossly unjust. The investment that the European Community is making in infrastructure, skill levels and direct development aids to industry is on behalf of every Irish person, not just of those already in employment.

79. Solidarity obliges Irish management and directors to be more open and accountable in the use that is made of whatever surplus

their companies generate, to actively pursue policies of job creation in Ireland and to accept remuneration levels that maintain a just proportion with what others elsewhere in the economy receive. It obliges Irish workers – and their trade unions – to assume their share of responsibility for the health and expansion of the enterprises employing them, to respect profoundly the use of the strike weapon[24] and similarly to guard a due proportion between the wages they demand for their work and the income levels of those who, through no fault of their own, cannot participate in the economy. Where management and trade unions in Ireland today are colluding in having a smaller workforce that is more highly paid (through, for example, regular and substantial overtime working, or the virtual purchase of redundancies), the virtue of solidarity is clearly absent. The amount of overtime that is regularly being worked in some parts of the economy is deeply disturbing because it seems to reject any responsibility at all for alleviating unemployment. Solidarity holds up a totally different ideal: '...the purpose of a business firm is not simply to make a profit but is to be found in its very existence as a *community of persons* who in various ways are endeavouring to satisfy their basic needs, and who form a particular group at the service of the whole of society' (*Centesimus Annus*, n.35).

80. Pope John Paul II has developed a concept which helps us to appreciate how widely shared is the responsibility for ensuring satisfactory levels of employment in a society. He speaks of the 'indirect employer' in order to refer to the way in which many individuals, groups and associations can, by their behaviour, influence the employment content of economic growth (*Laborem Exercens*, n.17). While an employer in the traditional sense is the person responsible for actually recruiting someone, the employer's ability to do so is powerfully conditioned by the myriad ways in which other actors and agencies can make it easy or difficult to employ an extra person. For example, heavy payroll taxes; burdensome legislation; rises in key living costs that employees must pay (eg. public transport, housing, etc.); measures by unions or professional associations that unduly limit the supply of qualified

personnel; hikes in interest rates; the abrupt revaluation of the pound *vis-à-vis* the currencies of key export markets, and so on, all constitute factors which an individual employer does not control but which powerfully condition his or her ease in employing further workers. Very many individuals and groups in Ireland today are, to an important degree, 'indirect employers'. Solidarity invites them to acknowledge this role and to appreciate that it commits them '...*to act against unemployment*, which in all cases is an evil, and which, when it reaches a certain level, can become a real social disaster' (*Laborem Exercens*, n.18).

REFERENCES

1   Some sources that provide a good window onto Catholic social teaching and its development are:

Gregory Baum, *The Priority of Labor: A Commentary on Laborem Exercens, Encyclical Letter of Pope John Paul II*, New York/Ramsey: Paulist Press, 1982;

Donal Dorr, *Option for the Poor: A Hundred Years of Vatican Social Teaching*, Dublin: Gill & Macmillan, 1983;

Jean-Yves Calvez and Jacques Perrin, *The Church and Social Justice: The Social Teaching of the Popes from Leo XIII to Pius XII, 1878-1958*, Chicago: Regnery, 1961;

Hervé Carrier, SJ, *The Social Doctrine of the Church Revisited: A Guide for Study*, Vatican City: Pontifical Council for Justice and Peace, 1990;

Joseph Gremillion (ed.), *The Gospel of Peace and Justice: Catholic Social Teaching since Pope John*, Maryknoll, New York: Orbis, 1976;

John Molony, *The Worker Question – A New Historical Perspective on Rerum Novarum*, Dublin: Gill & Macmillan, 1991;

Pontifical Council for Justice and Peace, *Human Rights and the Church: Historical and Theological Reflections,* Conferences presented at an International Colloquium, Rome, 14-16 November 1988, Vatican City: Pontifical Council for Justice and Peace, 1990;

Pontifical Council for Justice and Peace, *Social and Ethical Aspects of Economics, A Colloquium in the Vatican*, Vatican City: Pontifical Council for Justice and Peace, 1992;

Ways of Peace: Papal Messages for the World Days of Peace (1968-1986), Vatican City: Pontifical Council for Justice and Peace, 1986.

2 'Every human being has inalienable rights that must be respected. Each human community – ethnic, historical, cultural or religious – has rights which must be respected. Peace is threatened every time one of these rights is violated.'

'As long as injustices exist in any of the areas that touch upon the dignity of the human person, be it in the political, social or economic field, be it in the cultural or religious sphere, true peace will not exist. The causes of inequalities must be identified through a courageous and objective evaluation, and they must be eliminated so that every person can develop and grow in the full measure of his or her humanity' (Address of Pope John Paul II at Drogheda, 29 September 1979, in *The Pope in Ireland: Addresses and Homilies*, Dublin: Veritas Publications, 1979, n.8, pp.20-21).

3 Many individuals and organisations are seeking to protect rights such as '...the right to be born, the right to life, the

right to responsible procreation, to work, to peace, to freedom and social justice, the right to participate in the decisions that affect people and nations...' and are active in combating '...various forms of collective violence like discrimination against individuals and groups, the use of physical and psychological torture perpetrated against prisoners or political dissenters' *(John Paul II in Mexico, His Collected Speeches*, London: Collins, 1979, p.80).

4   For example, Mk 3:1-6; Lk 12:37-46; Mk 10:13-16; Lk 9:37-42.

5   Pope John Paul II, *Redemptor Hominis (Redeemer of Man)*, 4 March 1979, London: Catholic Truth Society.

6   Vatican II, *Gaudium et Spes (Pastoral Constitution on the Church in the Modern World)*, 7 December 1965, in Walter M. Abbott SJ (General Editor), *The Documents of Vatican II*, London: Geoffrey Chapman, 1966.

7   See also *Centesimus Annus*, n.6; *Libertatis Conscientia*, nn.82-86; *Gaudium et Spes*, n.34.

8   Congregation for the Doctrine of the Faith, *Libertatis Conscientia (Instruction on Christian Freedom and Liberation)*, 22 March 1986, London: Catholic Truth Society.

9   *Rerum Novarum, Encyclical Letter of Pope Leo XIII on the Conditions of the Working Classes*, Study Edition: A New Translation with Introduction and Notes by Joseph Kirwan, London: Catholic Truth Society, 1983.

10   Research into poverty in the South, in 1987, found that denying a head of household's right to work, or setting a low value on it, explained the poverty of some 70 per cent

of all households in poverty. Thus, of the total of poor households, 34 per cent were headed by an unemployed person, 24 per cent by a small farmer, and 10 per cent by an employee. (Callan *et al*, op. cit., Table 7.11, p.104)

11 See 'The Incentive to Work' in The Council for Social Welfare, *Unemployment, Jobs and the 1990s*, op. cit., paras.16-17, pp.8-9.

12 Pope John Paul II, Address at Cuilapan, Mexico, 29 January 1979, in *John Paul II in Mexico: His Collected Speeches*, op. cit., p.96.

13 '...property is acquired first of all through work in order that it may serve work. This concerns in a special way ownership of the means of production. ...They cannot be *possessed against labour*, they cannot even be *possessed for possession's sake*, because the **only legitimate title to their possession** ... is *that they should serve labour*, and thus by serving labour, that they should make possible the achievement of the ... (fundamental principle of the moral order), namely, the universal destination of goods and the right to common use of them' (*Laborem Exercens*, n.14, emphasis added).

'Ownership of the means of production, whether in industry or agriculture, is just and legitimate if it serves useful work. It becomes illegitimate, however, when it is not utilised or when it serves to impede the work of others, in an effort to gain a profit which is not the result of the overall expansion of work and the wealth of society, but rather is the result of curbing them or of illicit exploitation, speculation or the breaking of solidarity among working people.

'...ownership (of the means of production) morally justifies itself in the creation, at the proper time and in the proper way, of opportunities for work and human growth for all' (*Centesimus Annus*, n.43).

14   Pope John Paul II, *Sollicitudo Rei Socialis (The Social Concern of the Church)*, 30 December 1987, London: Catholic Truth Society.

15   Pope Paul VI, *Populorum Progressio (The Development of Peoples)*, 26 March 1967, London: Catholic Truth Society.

16   See 'Authentic Human Development', Part IV of *Sollicitudo Rei Socialis*.

17   See paragraphs 47-53.

18   See *Gaudium et Spes*, n.65;

US National Conference of Catholic Bishops, *Economic Justice for All: Pastoral Letter on Catholic Social Teaching and the US Economy*, Washington DC: United States Catholic Conference, 1986, n.15; nn.71-72.

19   For example, see *Populorum Progressio*, n.33.

20   See *Populorum Progressio*, n.19.

21   Consult Chapter 1 in Richard Douthwaite, *The Growth Illusion*, Dublin: Lilliput Press, 1992.

22   'Left to themselves, market forces favour the wealthy, the strong and the powerful, and hurt or even crush the poor, the weak and the powerless. A Christian society must provide safety nets of justice and compassion to protect the weaker sectors from the destructive consequences of uncontrolled market forces' (Cardinal Cahal B. Daly, Sermon, St Bartholomew's Church, Dublin, 23 August 1992).

23 For a discussion of the moral issues raised by the operation of the market, see Cardinal Cahal B. Daly, op. cit.

24 'Certain questions must be asked by all those involved before a strike is begun:

   1. Is it sure that a real injustice is present?
   2. Is this injustice grave enough to justify the loss and damage likely to be caused?
   3. Is there a proper proportion between the loss about to be inflicted and the lawful end pursued?
   4. Have all efforts been made to reach settlement by negotiation, and have these efforts failed?

   A person involved in a strike decision must be able to answer these questions in the affirmative before he can say: "This strike is morally justified". We must not forget that a strike is a weapon of last resort and can never be the first move in a dispute' (*The Work of Justice: Irish Bishops' Pastoral*, op. cit., para.72, p.35).

PART THREE

The Application: Analyses and Policy Responses to Date

81. People will ask: "How can such values be expressed? When will we know that we are living by them?" So far we have given some examples of what these fundamental values look like in practice[1] but only with a view to explaining the values themselves. Now we want to explore more fully what living by them involves in Ireland today.

82. It is possible for people who sincerely hold the same value to differ in their opinions as to which policy, in the circumstances of today, is the best embodiment of that value. We are aware of this. In the preceding section, in direct fulfilment of our teaching role as bishops, we outlined fundamental values that are **inherent** in the Christian vision of the human person. But that does not exhaust our responsibilities as pastors. We have to lead our Christian communities in analysing '...the situation which is proper to their own country, to shed on it the light of the Gospel's unalterable words and to draw principles of reflection, **norms of judgement and directives for action** from the social teaching of the Church' (*Octogesima Adveniens*, n.4, emphasis added).[2]

83. Here we share some judgements, and indicate lines of action, which we see as essential to ensuring work for everyone in Ireland today. But, though carefully arrived at, these judgements and recommended lines of action remain fallible. We ask our own faithful, however, and all others on this island, to reflect seriously on what we say, and to make their own contribution so that a common vision might unite us.[3] What is happening to unemployed people is far too serious for us to regard judgements as to what is to be done as purely personal and private affairs.

(i) Improving our Economic Stewardship

84. We begin by observing that the responsibility for creating more jobs on this island lies, first of all, in **Irish** hands. We welcome

those analyses which have refused to sanction a fatalistic outlook or to lay the blame for our high unemployment and emigration at the door of 'Brussels' or the 'world economy'.[4]

85. Irish people are tempted to shrug off the challenge of unemployment with observations that effectively distance them from responsibility for what is happening. For example, they point out that it is an international problem. However, what many other industrial countries regard as a 'problem' is an unemployment rate **one half** the Irish rate.[5] Or they like to observe that technology is to blame. They fail to explain, however, how it is that other, small, open economies have much **more advanced** technology than Ireland and yet much lower unemployment rates (for example, the Nordic countries). A third observation that is sometimes made is that this island is on the periphery of Europe. But countries like Finland, on the northern edge of the continent, and Japan, on the periphery of Asia, have not let geography stand in the way of their economic development.[6]

86. A fourth observation which is frequently cited is that our rapid population growth of the recent past has made high unemployment inevitable in the present. Some people are even of the opinion that we shall have to 'ride out' the high unemployment and emigration of today until population change in the next century brings a fall in the number of young people entering the labour market. We believe that this shirks the challenge and the opportunity for better economic development that the number of qualified young people knocking on the door of our economy and society constitutes. When included in our places of work, their openness and learning enable new work practices and technologies to be more rapidly assimilated. As consumers they expand the domestic market; when they are PAYE earners, they help bring down the exceptionally high dependency ratio that Irish workers currently bear;[7] as citizens they increase the vitality of our social and political life. It is a cause of deep concern to us, therefore, when our young people are spoken of, no longer as our greatest

national asset, but as a major cause of our high unemployment. This is to assume wrongly that everything possible is being done and that the energy and skills of these young people are simply surplus to our country's requirements.

87. Each of those observations, therefore, draws attention to a factor with which we have to reckon, but not to something which we should regard as a full stop or a crippling handicap. We should feel challenged by the better employment performance of other small, European countries.[8] They ride the same ups and downs in the international economy and have to cope with the same advancing technology as we do. They have had increasing levels of participation by women and inflows of migrant workers. Their unemployment rates, however, have been consistently lower than what we have in Ireland. Greater knowledge of their stewardship of their economic resources can powerfully expose Irish special pleading.

88. The countries to which we refer are in no way homogeneous. They prove that the survival of native culture, including language and institutions, is wholly compatible with good economic management and even depends upon it. Irish cultural and spiritual values should in no way feel threatened, therefore, by the challenge of improving our economic stewardship.

89. The scope for further economic development and job creation on this island is far from exhausted. Until it has been, we cannot describe our unemployment levels as inevitable or as the responsibility of 'Brussels'. While every new policy measure is a source of hope, and deserves full support unless it proves itself unworthy of it, we feel that each of the following examples of poor stewardship of Irish economic resources loses its validity only when the problem is gone and not simply because a new policy to address it has been announced. These examples are not original; placing them together, however, helps to underline the extent to which genuine economic development is an unfinished task.[9]

● The value added to agricultural raw materials by further processing is low by the standards of other European countries. This state of affairs coexists with, and is partially caused by, an agricultural sector that has relied to a greater extent upon selling into intervention than the agricultural sector of any other member state in the EC. There is the potential for this island to be home to some of Europe's major food companies.[10]

● Sectors of manufacturing industry are so overwhelmingly made up of the branch plants of multinational corporations that dramatic growth rates in exports are giving only a relatively minor boost to the rest of the economy. This is because these branch plants import many of the materials they need and repatriate most of the profits they generate. The sub-supply companies that would help integrate these multinationals more into the economy of this island have not been forthcoming in the numbers required.[11]

● Nothing is so home-made as the present taxation system in the Republic and yet it is acknowledged as one of the biggest obstacles to better progress in job creation. Companies find that a variety of policies reduce the cost of using capital while other policies add to the cost of employing people. A now infamous 'tax wedge' makes it difficult for employers to reward hard-working, single people as it is liable to cost them nearly £2 to ensure their employee receives an extra £1. Ireland is a society whose taxation system is benign on capital and harsh on labour.[12]

● Since the early 1960s, successive reports and policy supports have tried to address those weaknesses in Irish management which would be exposed by growing international competition. Yet Irish management still remains weak in international marketing, in its ability to harness technological advances to the task of product innovation, in its formulation of business strategy and in its fostering of dynamic relationships with its employees. Employment gains by multinationals since Ireland joined the European

Community have been offset by the redundancies in companies under Irish management. How many of the companies under its direction will flourish in the Single Market?

• There is no shortage of either domestic savings or foreign currency for investment in our island's economy. Domestic savings in the Republic and its net earnings of foreign currency (the balance of payments surplus) are remarkably high by international standards but these funds are not finding their way into job-creating investment. For example, though all this money is in the financial system, small and medium sized businesses, whose role in economic development is widely recognised as crucial, are still finding it extraordinarily difficult to get venture capital.

• A single market is still far from being a reality on this island. There is considerable evidence that each part of Ireland is importing from outside the island goods and services that are available from companies in the other part.[13] It is wholly compatible with being good Europeans to look for opportunities to strengthen existing companies and to create new ones by regarding this island's five million people as the one market.

• Ireland has a strong case at the level of the European Community for assistance in regional and rural development. The need, however, is not just for particular **levels** of funding but for **ways** of using the funding that are, in fact, effective in raising sustainable employment levels and furthering our economic development. While Ireland continues to press the EC to take responsibility for an adequate level of funding, it is an Irish responsibility to identify ways of using it which see it fulfils its intended purpose.

• While there is an evident scarcity of jobs on this island, there is no shortage of work to be done – in renewing urban areas, caring for the specialised needs of vulnerable groups in the population, bringing health services and educational and training opportunities up to the standards of other small but more dynamic countries, improving public transportation systems, conserving our environment and historical heritage, making our prison system more humane, and so much more. The challenge to us as a people is to give greater priority to these needs by putting resources into meeting them.

Our purpose in drawing attention to these instances of poor stewardship is to show why we believe it is **not true** that everything possible is being done about unemployment. It is not our intention to sketch a programme for job creation but to awaken a fresh interest in completing the economic development of this island. As a people, we are morally obliged by the large number of people seeking jobs to move from mediocrity to excellence in the stewardship of our economic resources. The challenge of building a stronger economy on this island is primarily one to our solidarity with each other and to the intelligence of our policies. We should complain more about our lack of social cohesion and our policy failures, and less about technology and the numbers of our young people.

90. The challenge particularly concerns Government. It is true that the State could only guarantee every citizen a job if it were to control practically every aspect of economic and social life, a cure that would be worse than the disease. It is just as unacceptable, however, that the State be confined to the polar opposite role, namely one where it has no responsibility at all for job creation but merely protects the rights of property and capital. It is deeply disheartening to people concerned about the jobs issue when the extent of new action by the social partners appears to be exhausted by the commissioning of a further report rather than acting on already established findings, by the announcement of new schemes and labour market measures when more than a decade of such experimentation has done very little to remedy the unemployment problem, or by the establishment of yet another body to discuss the issue and advise. In Ireland today a clear, long-term programme for job-creation (and not simply for economic growth or fiscal stability) needs to be decided upon **and implemented**,

and Irish people expect the State to play the leading role in this and to secure the wide co-operation necessary.

(ii) Widening and Deepening a Consensus on Jobs

91. While we welcome the honesty and humility of analyses that remind us of how much is in our Irish hands – our sometimes incompetent and unwilling hands – we also acknowledge and appreciate the considerable progress that has been made. Productivity and efficiency in nearly every sector of the economy, from agriculture to financial services, are incomparably greater now than thirty years ago.

92. In particular, the Republic's economy shows a commendable soundness under several headings (low inflation, strong balance of payments, new control over the public finances and the national debt). These are considerable achievements when we recall how relatively recently there was cause for deep concern under each heading. The turn-arounds that have been effected serve to underline what **can** be done when a political and social consensus develops. However, while necessary, this financial soundness is not a sufficient condition for reducing unemployment. Rather than resting content with the improvement in monetary variables, therefore, we should be led on to plan and implement a real onslaught on unemployment.

93. An important part of the Republic's success in stemming the deterioration in its public finances was its discovery of what the smaller, European democracies learned before it, and learned better: in a small, trading economy, key actors cannot afford to have widely different views on how the economy is to be run. Our solidarity as a people has to find better institutions and procedures if we are to work together to develop the skills of our people and the resources of this island in the interests of everyone.

94. The smallness of our economy and society poses dangers and an opportunity here. One danger is that a relatively small group of

people can engage in trading favours so as to cement their privilege and power. Another danger is that, when confrontation replaces negotiation in our industrial relations, the economy's trading ability is so damaged that overall income contracts sharply and there are no winners, only losers all around. Smallness, however, also presents an opportunity. It is grasped when vision and a commitment to the common good enable intelligent strategies to be developed and pursued to capture even a small increase in world market share, as this can bring a huge rise in national income.

95. The Central Review Group set up under the Programme for Economic and Social Progress[14] in the Republic is a good beginning but, if a really effective consensus is to be created, more is needed. The search should be for ways to widen the consultation mechanisms which have been built so as to include the Oireachtas, the voluntary sector and the unemployed. The process should also be deepened by extending the consultation back into the individual firm because, after all, it is on the quality of the co-operation between management and workers that so much of our economic health depends.

(iii) Business Enterprise

96. It appears to us that one of the most important things around which consensus needs to be built today is the role of business enterprise. This is because the economic development of this island can never be done **for** us. It can only be done **by** us.[15] Neither multinationals nor the European Community can hand us a resilient, modern economy which is able to generate its own employment growth and change. Either we build that ourselves, with the judiciously selected support of multinationals, foreign banks and the EC, or we will remain an economy that permanently frustrates the job-aspirations of Irish people. There is now a welcome emphasis on the role that indigenous industry must play and, thus, on the contribution that Irish people have to make as managers and entrepreneurs. Never has it been so necessary that

women and men of talent apply themselves to the challenge of creating and running internationally trading companies that put down deep roots in the rest of the economy.

97. There is evidence that an unduly large number of bright and talented people in Ireland pursue handsome fees and salaries by acting as consultants in tax, legal and property matters. The incentive system at work here is clearly not serving our country as it should. It is rewarding those who master the intricacies of the Irish tax and legal systems more than those who create or expand employment. It means that talented people who might otherwise have been involved in direct job creation are diverted into this form of entrepreneurship. In this context, the simplification of the tax code, the dismantling of restrictive practices in the legal and other professions, and the setting of limits to the profits to be made from land speculation, can each make a contribution to the expansion of employment in Ireland. It would release needed talent, energy and resources to the demanding task of widening our industrial base and creating stronger Irish companies.[16]

98. The fostering and encouragement of the entrepreneurship that creates jobs is a responsibility that must be widely shared – by parents, by our educational system (in particular, schools of business studies); by those who design our taxation code and industrial support policies; by employers' bodies and trade unions; and by all who help shape public opinion. It must be clear that we cannot want jobs without also wanting more of that type of person whose energy and drive helps create them. To want a culture not dominated by the economy (paras. 67-71) does not mean setting our face against an enterprising economy.

99. The need for people of enterprise has been sharpened by the growing integration of the two economies in Ireland with the rest of the European Community. In the first place, if national authorities increasingly align their instruments of macroeconomic policy such as exchange rates, interest rates and tax rates with those prevailing throughout the Community, the quality of the micro-

economic decisions being made at sectoral and company level will assume greater and greater importance. Put more simply, national central banks and finance ministers will be less and less able to produce major boosts to job creation (such as cuts in interest rates, or the introduction of tax incentives) so that more and more will depend on the quality of the investment and business decisions being made by individual companies. The rewards for efficiency and the penalties for inefficiency at company level are becoming greater than ever as the Single Market takes effect. Every Irish company or consumer has had the experience of admiring some new product from overseas for its design, ingeniousness, quality, cheapness or whatever. We should want that overseas companies and consumers regularly find themselves admiring an Irish product for a similar reason.

100. It is also important to realise how much it depends on the business community if benefits are to accrue to the whole community from the Structural Funds' expenditure currently being made by the EC. It constitutes a major investment in the island of Ireland by the Community. The return on this investment, however, to both the people of Ireland and to the EC as a whole, will crucially depend on the willingness and ability of more individuals and companies to seize the better opportunities **to trade from Ireland** that all this investment is bringing about.

101. Fostering business enterprise need not lead to greater selfishness, rampant greed and inequalities of wealth. A Christian understanding of enterprise sees that freedom of economic initiative for the individual is important for the common good also (*Sollicitudo Rei Socialis*, n.15). The intelligence and talents of an individual can motivate and mobilise collective undertakings through which many people collaborate to their mutual benefit and the enhancement of their society (*Centesimus Annus*, n.32). It should be a source of deep personal satisfaction to entrepreneurs in Ireland today to know that their energy and drive enable other people also to participate in economic life and to experience the dignity of earning.

102. The bond between business entrepreneurs and the rest of society is weakened when some of them flaunt personal life styles of excessive consumption which appear to constitute them a race apart from their fellow citizens. Such dangerous illusions are encouraged by the adulatory attention accorded by some of our media to the 'doings' of the wealthy. While it is true that Irish people need to abandon any lingering cultural suspicion or resentment of the woman or man who breaks new ground and grows wealthy because of it, people, nevertheless, are right to expect business leaders to lead lives which are purposeful to themselves and to the nation as a whole. In this way, the young could appreciate that business is an occupation, like others, through which the community is served.

103. It further endangers our social fabric when individuals use their entrepreneurial talents to amass fortunes which owe more to clever changes in the multiple ways in which money can be held, or to the manipulation of tax codes or other legislative arrangements, than to activity which creates jobs. Complex tax and company laws, combined with the increasing scale and globalisation of financial markets, have created opportunities for larger and more sophisticated abuses than could be imagined in the past in Ireland. The social damage that can now be wrought by the immoral business person is correspondingly greater. Fraud and misappropriation are never victimless crimes. The ability of the economy to generate jobs – and, as a result, the quality of life for unemployed people – is at stake.

104. Every effort should be made to develop techniques of control and surveillance that keep pace with the opportunities for dishonest gains. Yet it is important that people in business be guided by more than what the law does not forbid. They should value openness and be willing to see their decisions and gains reported publicly. They should also value solidarity and social love, being keen that how they use the resources they control should bring real benefits to the rest of society, especially its weakest members.

105. Ireland today cannot afford cynicism towards the role of business entrepreneurship. The tragedy of immoral business behaviour is that it erodes public esteem for the civic and social role of business generally. Irish people, if anything, need to be more understanding of those who fail honourably in business and to encourage them to try again rather than to judge all business failure harshly. We repeat: the person who creates an enterprise which enables people's work to come to the market-place has practised a genuine form of patriotism that is essential for today.

106. One characteristic institution through which enterprise is channelled is the publicly-owned commercial company. While it is true that the nature of the ownership of a company (whether it be foreign, private or public) is less important to its ability to create jobs in Ireland than, for example, the extent of its linkages with the rest of the economy or its ability to innovate new product lines and services, nevertheless, other things being equal, the publicly-owned company affords people an opportunity to put their business talents and energies directly at the service of their country. Semi-State companies played an important role in allowing people to do this in the early years of the Irish State. It is important to continue to respect and foster the special motivation which they can call forth. The memory of their pioneering work is being kept alive today in successful new ventures through which semi-State bodies are playing a full part in creating good jobs through their capacity for innovation.

107. The co-operative form of enterprise is another one which deserves particular support from the community at large. Through co-operative associations, people give exceptional expression to the communal nature of their work and, frequently, to their links with a local community. It appears to have been difficult to foster producer co-operatives on a significant scale in areas other than food and agriculture. Patient educational work, the possibility of fresh legislative supports, the strengthening of contacts with co-operative movements in other countries, and other measures, are

to be earnestly encouraged. When commercial enterprise flourishes within a formal co-operative framework, the full human context of economic activity is particularly transparent.[17]

(iv) Empowering Communities and Regions

108. It remains one of the most endearing and encouraging aspects of life on this island that people have a deep attachment to place. There is a pride in, and a willingness to work for, one's own area or community that is expressed in a wealth of community and voluntary associations. However, this attachment to place is being lived out in what are two of the most centralised States in Western Europe which, at present, accord local and regional autonomy very limited recognition.

109. In Northern Ireland, a political impasse brought its experience of regional autonomy to an end in 1972 and has resulted in a substantially weakened system of local government. In the Republic, abolition of rates on domestic dwellings in 1977 weakened a local government system that was already strongly in the hands of the national political parties. In our counties and towns, therefore, it is, sadly, people's experience that it is difficult to influence the development of their own hinterland and that you need to be in London or Dublin to do so. They feel that their involvement in decision-making is marginal. It is ironic that an island which needs to strengthen considerably the civic culture of its inhabitants should have two political systems which accord its citizens very limited opportunities to grow in the necessary virtues through the experience of involvement in local government. For example, local government in Northern Ireland handles about three per cent of total government expenditure and in the Republic about thirteen per cent. In Denmark, by contrast, the percentage is around seventy per cent.[18] The principle of subsidiarity[19] (leaving decisions to be made at the lowest level at which it is practicable to do so) needs to be honoured within Ireland and not just at the level of the European Community.

110. While the case for the reform of local government and the strengthening of regional authorities can be argued on several grounds, we wish to highlight – in the context of this Pastoral – its potential contribution to economic development and job creation.[20] Local knowledge, local commitment and local participation are key ingredients in all authentic development. The identification of business opportunities that build on local amenities and resources, and the application of the energy and skills needed to harness them, require a particular type of partnership between local people and outside agencies. The former need to be open to learning about the new opportunities and the new obstacles that a rapidly changing external environment is throwing up (the reform of the EC's Common Agricultural Policy, the Single European Market, shifts in the tourist market, new EC programmes to support rural development, etc.). The latter need to see their role as one of empowering and facilitating people to become more the subjects of their own development and of that of their area/region. Scattering branch offices through the regions, when policy formulation and control of its implementation remain the exclusive prerogatives of head office in the capital, does not harness energy at local level to the challenges of economic development and job creation.[21] However, when the relationships between a local community and outside agencies are based on openness and respect, real development can take place and an 'us and them' mentality is dissolved in the recognition of a common challenge and complementary strengths.[22]

111. We thank God that community and voluntary effort is very much alive. Many national and EC programmes rely on it for much of their take-up. In particularly deprived areas, it can happen that local organisations, balancing with considerable ingenuity different sources of funding, have become important generators of economic activity. They have, in effect, played the role of entrepreneurs in bringing about the provision of needed services in their own community (women's centres, child-care facilities, youth services, support to job-seekers and small businesses, hostels, etc.). The challenge is to facilitate them further in providing real

employment. Their efforts need to be treated with the utmost respect by the State and, where it is clear that no alternative jobs are available to the people in question, public funding should be structured to support them on a longer-term basis. In the context of the present scarcity of jobs in the private and public sectors, it makes little sense for the local groups' concentration on a medium or long-term project to be frustrated by the State's insistence that participants on schemes have to be changed each year. Payment levels should reflect the dignity of the labour of the people who take part in them and, at the same time, constitute a real incentive for them to do so.

112. We encourage district councils and local authorities, and health and educational committees, to explore creatively how they could use even the limited economic powers they **do** have to provide more job opportunities for unemployed people to take part in administering some of those services on which their own communities heavily depend.[23] Companies in the private sector also have a role to play. In Great Britain and the USA, some companies have formulated strategies for actively involving themselves as partners in the efforts of deprived communities and social groups to develop themselves. In Ireland, to date, it is largely business and professional people acting in a private capacity who have done this. Large companies, on the contrary, have been slow to formulate any policy on social responsibility, let alone on solidarity with unemployed people and their communities, which goes beyond corporate donations.[24]

113. There are encouraging examples of parishes and local communities which have taken initiatives to support unemployed people in finding their voice. Sometimes they have also taken a hand in creating jobs. Such solidarity with unemployed people is an important part of being a Christian community. We urge every parish and Christian community to show creativity and determination in bringing people together from every walk of life to forge a truly inclusive community where the rights of unemployed people are fully respected.

(v) Job Creation and the Environment

114. The evident excesses of the consumer society can lead to a sense of antipathy towards such things as economic growth, new technology, enterprise and market forces. It is true that when such things are not regulated and guided by a wider vision of human life and by institutionalised commitments to the common good, they spawn environmental degradation, increased unemployment and widening social inequality.

115. In Ireland we might well count our blessings when we compare our environment with that of supposedly 'richer' countries. A religious perspective on life should support the insight that the natural environment is not a limitless warehouse of cost-free materials but that its riches and resources are finite and a gift from a loving Creator to the whole human family (*Laborem Exercens*, n.12; *Centesimus Annus*, n.37). It is a heritage which we receive, ennobled by work, from the hands of previous generations and which we ought to hand on, enriched in turn by our work, to those who will live on this island after us.

116. The pursuit of greater employment opportunities for our people, with the economic growth which that requires, need not sacrifice the quality of our environment, although some alteration in the existing environment may sometimes be unavoidable. It is already clear that the relatively unspoilt environment of this island is important to our food and tourism industries. We should, in fact, hope to be able to provide a growing number of jobs **through** enhancing our environment – jobs in making the filters, treatment plants and other equipment our factories need, jobs in tending land, trees and our water resources, jobs in organic agriculture, waste recycling, urban renewal, and in so much else. Economic growth which reduces total employment or which leaves greater new needs in its wake (a damaged environment, burned-out people) is a run-away engine. Society, acting through its legislators, government, business community, labour

movement, and at every level, has to seek to influence what it is that grows and the way in which it grows so that economic growth genuinely benefits the human family, each member of it and its habitat.

(vi) Jobs and Europe

117. The debate on the Maastricht Treaty has brought many people to reflect, perhaps more deeply than ever before, on Ireland and Europe. The case was strongly put by many of those who argued for a 'yes' vote in the Republic's referendum on the Treaty, that the Union would bring even further financial inflows to Ireland.[25] To people who believed that our unemployed and emigrants had benefited little from the monies already received, this argument, however, was beside the point. To others it appeared to provide further proof that we were 'throwing ourselves' at Europe hoping that the Union would do for us what we were proving incapable of doing for ourselves.

118. Although unemployment is a problem throughout the EC, it is particularly serious in Ireland. Because of this, but even more because of the universal values to which we called attention in Part Two of this Pastoral, we believe that Ireland's voice needs to be heard strongly within the European Community calling attention to the importance of a practical and effective commitment to jobs.

119. This is not simply to seek larger financial transfers. It is to play a constructive role in the debate about the type of Europe the Community would like to see develop. Persistent high unemployment damages the European Community in the same way as it damages Ireland – undermining the Community's social cohesion, civic culture and the credibility of its world role. Ireland's experience in this regard needs to be listened to at the Community level. This means that it is not just a narrow Irish interest but a concern for the quality of any future European Union which makes it important to guard against an over-emphasis on monetary objec-

tives in the present movement towards economic and monetary union (EMU). Even a stable, single currency throughout the Union would not be sufficient European support for our employment objectives. This island would need a Union which could ensure low interest rates and steady economic growth, as well as fiscal transfers on a realistic scale. We welcome the growing European consciousness on this island and the participation of so many Irish people in building a more united Europe.

120. The debate on the Maastricht Treaty has also generated an increased awareness among many Irish people that the development of the European Community is not just about economics. It is about the type of life and society which we want on this island and about the contribution that all the participating States can collectively make, through the Community, to a safer and more just world for all peoples. Harmonisation and mutual enrichment are not absorption. Building a new Europe does not mean an uncritical acceptance of a movement towards a new superstate. It is a matter of trying to bring the positive human and Christian values of our Irish tradition into dialogue with the values of the other communities with whom we constitute the present 'Community'.[26] In this dialogue, we will have much to learn which can enrich and improve our society but we should also believe that we have positive things to say, things which can enrich and improve other societies.

(vii) Justice While Unemployed

121. Even dramatic progress by our society in wanting, and effectively seeking, a better employment performance from our economy would not lessen immediate and pressing moral obligations arising from the present level of unemployment. Justice requires that we do all that is in our power, now, to change decisively the experience of being unemployed even while we commit ourselves wholeheartedly to job creation.

122. This means accepting and protecting the rights of unemployed people. In the first place, unemployed people are entitled to adequate compensation for their unemployment, that is, to an income which keeps them and their dependants out of poverty. While rising unemployment inevitably brings a rising social welfare bill, the transfer of that income should be a 'non-negotiable' in our political life. We are dealing with the income on which people are expected to live and it is unhelpful and one-sided to speak of it purely as a 'cost', or financial 'burden'. They too are taxpayers as, typically, their entire incomes are spent and incur value-added tax. It is important that people be aware of the different uses to which tax revenue is put so as not to attribute in a simplistic way their high personal taxation to the number of people receiving unemployment compensation. For example, in the Republic, tax reliefs which benefit almost exclusively people in employment cost a sizeable sum each year.[27] This public support to them is less visible than the social security paid to unemployed people. Just as it is unthinkable that the Government should neglect to pay its employees properly or to service the national debt so it should be unthinkable that it seek to provide anything other than an adequate income to those people who are unable to find jobs. New surges in unemployment should not panic our society into any whittling away of the entitlements of unemployed people.[28]

123. Unemployed people are entitled to the administration of unemployment compensation in a way that is courteous and respectful. In Northern Ireland, as throughout the United Kingdom, unemployed people have been subject for over a decade to repeated changes in the rules governing their entitlement to social security. They have experienced this as a growing unwillingness on the part of the rest of society to provide adequate support. In the Republic, while the numbers who must depend on unemployment compensation have increased fourfold since the late 1970s, staffing and facilities to serve them have only expanded marginally so that, in some instances, the circumstances surrounding payment remain degrading. Regrettably, cases of abrupt and insensitive treatment continue. Unemployed people claiming

payments are entitled to the same standards and courtesy as, for example, those that people expect from private financial institutions which handle their money.

124. People who have been unemployed for a long time are entitled to targeted and specialised assistance in finding a job once again. It has become accepted that, after unemployment has lasted a long time, it begins to feed on itself. In other words, individuals can lose confidence, work habits and skills to such an extent that when vacancies occur they are not even considered for them. Even substantial growth in the national economy passes them by. People in this situation need particular supports in order to escape from a state of 'unemployability',[29] just as everything needs to be done to prevent any more of the short-term unemployed from falling into such a trap in the first place. It is encouraging to see the recognition that is now being given the particular problem of long-term unemployment.

125. The rights we have been discussing of people who are unemployed carry corresponding obligations. Unemployed men and women are under an obligation – in the first place to their own humanity, and then to the rest of society – to do what they can to further improve and equip themselves for participation in economic life. This can take the form of catching up on education and involvement in training and personal development courses. If they already have skills and knowledge, they should, in so far as circumstances permit (and these can sometimes be very limiting, especially financially), seek to lead active rather than passive lives, participating in community or voluntary work or developing new talents and interests. They can opt to be more fully engaged in parenting and homeminding. Sometimes it has been the ability of a couple to successfully renegotiate roles when unemployment has been thrust upon them that has done most to mitigate its negative consequences.

126. The high unemployment of the 1980s brought public authorities to introduce a variety of special labour market measures with the intention of doing something additional about unemploy-

ment. There is deep dissatisfaction with aspects of these schemes among many unemployed people: the fact that all too often only the dole awaits them when their period on a scheme ends; the fact that they fall between the two stools of full social welfare protection and full legal entitlements as employees; the fact that often the schemes provide little or no training; the lack of a financial incentive to take part in them – at times, indeed, the incurring of a financial penalty for doing so.[30] We believe that the experience of participants should be more closely listened to and allowed to influence the design and implementation of all special labour market measures. Greater determination is needed on the part of the 'social partners', and closer co-operation with the community and voluntary sector, to ensure that these schemes do not constitute 'poor jobs for poor people'. The underlying motivation must be the good of people who are unemployed and never the political need to be 'seen to be doing something'.

127. Unemployed people are under an obligation to practise honesty and fairness in their dealings with the social welfare and tax authorities. That is how they expect to be treated themselves. There are instances of people who are unemployed enjoying relatively high living standards through their having succumbed to the temptation of untaxed money. They have some regular income which is not declared to the social welfare authorities. They are not alone in this. The likelihood is that the bulk of the work being done in the black economy is by people with jobs.[31] That jobholders may be the greatest sinners does not mean, however, that reforms should not be pursued which minimise the incentives to abuse unemployment compensation. Fraudulent drawing of the dole makes all unemployed people more vulnerable to suspicion and increased surveillance. The most important lines of reform include ensuring that what society gives people as their weekly income is adequate for them to live on;[32] ensuring that when people do take jobs that are available they do not become worse off;[33] and applying the 'availability for work' criterion in a humane way that recognises that unemployed people need to lead interesting and worthwhile lives even while being jobless.

128. We encourage all those who work in public training and placement agencies and in the administration of unemployment compensation to see themselves as allies of unemployed people in finding and facilitating some expression of their vocation to work. It is easy to give symptoms of unemployment (for example, low energy and poor time-keeping) the status of causes and to begin to think that people will remain the passive recipients of cash transfers indefinitely. A punitive or policing mentality, however, is counter-productive as it inevitably generates resistance rather than free co-operation. Imagination and courage are needed to find alternative ways in which society can help unemployed people to lead active and fulfilling lives. It will require active listening, repeated consultation and flexibility in the administration of publicly-provided benefits and schemes. There appears, in fact, to be considerable scope to change a largely passive approach to the needs of unemployed people into a more active one. We believe the search for a way forward must be based on the values we have outlined in Part Two of this Pastoral.

(viii) Any Job is not Better than None

129. Just as the State must not allow the scale of unemployment today to justify less humane treatment of the individuals who are unemployed, so employers must not allow the numbers seeking work to be a pretext for changing good jobs into bad ones.

130. Every responsible employer, and not just workers and their trade unions, regards 'poverty wages' as intolerable. Poorly paid workers become bad workers. Poor pay is a wholly inadequate foundation for any business to build on to ensure its profitability. Public authorities are also right to be deeply concerned about the phenomenon, for low pay damages human health and well-being, undermines the human capital of the economy by reducing workers' skills and flexibility, and strikes at the incentive to work of all unemployed people. Every job should be a bulwark against poverty. It is inconsistent to expect the State to supplement low wages

(Family Income Supplement in the Republic and Family Credit in Northern Ireland bring a topping-up payment to low paid workers with dependants), or to compensate for them (low incomes trigger eligibility criteria for many State social supports), while simultaneously denying it any right to veto how low wages can go. A Christian society has to concern itself with the question of a minimum wage. However it is ensured, no person's capacity for work should be treated by any employer as undeserving of what is commonly regarded as an acceptable wage.

131. A more complex phenomenon is the rapid spread of different types of work contract which are now termed 'atypical'. These include part-time working, fixed term contracts, sub-contracting, home-based work and the use of agency staff.[34] In addition, there is a growth in the number of people switching from employee status to self-employment.

132. Viewed positively, these new forms of work contract may give some people greater choice and flexibility to work as and when they prefer. They can be one way in which the benefits of the new information technologies serve to put the human person back in control. They can also serve to increase the flexibility of the labour market and facilitate more rapid economic growth. Viewed negatively, however, these developments may be used single-mindedly as cost-control exercises by employers, including public bodies. Then they give rise to a dual labour market. They accentuate the division within large enterprises between core and peripheral employees. The core is made up of full-time staff on good salaries, to whom the company is committed and provides ongoing training opportunities, workers it is reluctant to let go. The periphery is made up of 'replaceable' workers on temporary and/or part-time contracts, or not on the company's payroll at all but on that of a sub-contractor, for whom the company feels no real responsibility and whom it pays as little as possible. These developments need to be monitored closely and their longer-term consequences for the economy and society understood.

133. Women bear most of the insecurity produced by these 'atypical' work contracts. One regrettable feature of the high unemployment on this island is that it is partly responsible for Irish women having one of the lowest participation rates in paid employment in the European Community. We believe strongly that the role of a mother full-time in the home is a work deserving of the highest esteem – as indeed is that of a father where this occurs. We also believe, however, that this role should be freely assumed and that women should not be forced by barriers in the labour market to remain at home. These barriers include the fact that women bear the brunt of low pay, constitute the vast majority of part-time workers, face many situations where no provision at all is made for child-care, and have seen their relative pay level stagnate at approximately two-thirds of men's earnings in recent years. It is unacceptable that women's role in the work-force should bear the brunt of employers' attempts to control costs and public authorities' desire to control growth in the Live Register. It is also unacceptable that mothers who wish to work full-time in their homes should be driven by an inadequate family income to take up employment.

134. It is an enormous challenge facing employers, workers, trade unions and the public authorities to find ways of minimising the harm and of maximising the benefits of the proliferating 'atypical' forms of work. The task is crucial, however, to the health of our economies and to the cohesion of our societies. There will be little reason to be proud of greater flexibility in the labour market if that constitutes simply removing the safety net from under the most vulnerable.

> '...profitability is not the only indicator of a firm's condition. It is possible for the financial accounts to be in order, yet for the people – who make up the firm's most valuable asset – to be humiliated and their dignity offended. Besides being morally inadmissible, this will eventually have negative repercussions on the firm's economic efficiency. In fact, the purpose of a business firm is not simply to make a profit,

but is to be found in its very existence as **a community of persons** who in various ways are endeavouring to satisfy their basic needs, and who form a particular group at the service of the whole of society' (*Centesimus Annus*, n.35, emphasis added).

REFERENCES

1   See paragraphs 51, 56-57, 60, 68-69, 73, 76-79.

2   Pope Paul VI, *Octogesima Adveniens (The Eightieth Anniversary)*, 15 May 1971, London: Catholic Truth Society.

3   For a discussion on 'the movement from principle to policy' see US National Conference of Catholic Bishops, *Economic Justice For All: Pastoral Letter on Catholic Social Teaching and the US Economy*, op. cit., Chapter III, nn.134-135.

4   Some examples include:

   Industrial Policy Review Group, *A Time for Change: Industrial Policy for the 1990s* (The Culliton Report), Dublin: Stationery Office, 1992;

   Northern Ireland Economic Council, *Economic Strategy in Northern Ireland*, Belfast: Northern Ireland Economic Development Office, 1991 (Report 88);

   K.A. Kennedy, T. Giblin and D. McHugh, *The Economic Development of Ireland in the Twentieth Century*, London and New York: Routledge, 1988;

   National Economic and Social Council, *Ireland in the European Community: Performance, Prospects and Strategy*, Dublin: National Economic and Social Council, 1989 (Report No.88);

National Economic and Social Council, *A Strategy for the Nineties: Economic Stability and Structural Change*, Dublin: National Economic and Social Council, 1990 (Report No.89).

5 The US Bishops, for example, regarded unemployment as the most basic area of the US economic life demanding attention in their 1986 Pastoral Letter because it had developed to a 6 per cent rate, a level which '...would have been intolerable twenty years ago' (US National Conference of Catholic Bishops, op. cit., Chapter I, n.15).

6 Finland's average unemployment rate over the period 1980-1989 was 4.9 per cent, Japan's was 2.5 per cent, whereas Ireland's was 15.2 per cent! (OECD, *Employment Outlook*, July 1991, Paris: Organisation for Economic Co-operation and Development, Table 2.7, p.40)

7 In 1991, for example, every ten people in jobs in the Republic had some twenty-two other people depending on them, in Northern Ireland it was twenty, whereas, by comparison, every ten Danish job-holders had only nine.

8 In the period 1968-1973, Ireland's average employment growth rate was the lowest of the following countries – Austria, Denmark, Finland, Ireland, the Netherlands, Norway, Sweden, Switzerland; in the period 1973-1979, our growth rate in employment moved temporarily to third place, behind that of Norway and Sweden (this was due to massive borrowing that quickly proved unsustainable); in the 1980s, Ireland's employment growth returned to being the lowest of the group (OECD, op. cit., Table 2.5, p.36).

9 Part of the difficulty in preparing this Pastoral, and Part Three in particular, was that dramatic new events continued to affect the international and Irish economies, each one generating fresh uncertainties and, sometimes, provoking new policy measures or accelerating the introduction of

measures already talked about. Thus, for example, concerned people will follow closely the implementation and workings of the new £150m. equity fund for supporting expansions and start-ups by small businesses and which is to be managed on a county basis (announced August 1992). They will, similarly, follow carefully the implementation of whatever findings come out of the joint research project between the Northern Ireland Economic Research Centre (NIERC) and the Economic and Social Research Institute of the Republic (ESRI) on ways and means to bond the two economies on this island more closely together (inaugurated September 1992). Generally, progress in implementing the Culliton Report, and the fruits of doing so, should be a matter of intense public concern.

10 *A Time for Change: Industrial Policy for the 1990s* (The Culliton Report) has a special appendix on the Republic's food industry. It pleads for more vision, co-operation and co-ordination to unite the different sectors of the agricultural and food industry. (See Industrial Policy Review Group, op. cit., Appendix, 'The Food Industry', pp.87-104.) The Northern Ireland Economic Council suggests a similar policy approach for the food industry in Northern Ireland, adding an emphasis on the need for mergers in order to obtain economies of scale. (See Northern Ireland Economic Council, *The Food Processing Industry in Northern Ireland*, Belfast: Northern Ireland Economic Development Office, 1992, Report 92.)

11 There is evidence that the backward linkages of the foreign sector as whole (i.e. the inputs it buys from other sectors of the economy) have been weakening significantly, rather than strengthening, in recent years. The Central Bank's 1991 submission to the Industrial Policy Review Group substantiates this. (See The Central Bank, *Submission on Industrial Policy: A Report to the Industrial Policy Review Group*, Dublin: Stationery Office, 1992, pp.27-35.)

12   Chapter 4 of the Culliton Report concludes: 'In no other single area does the Government have at its disposal the tools to make as far-reaching and effective a reform to support an enterprise economy as in taxation' (Industrial Policy Review Group, op. cit., p.41).

An OECD study on marginal tax rates (published Autumn 1986) found that no other of the 24 OECD countries had a tax system as biased against the use of labour as the Irish. (Cited in The Central Bank, op. cit., p.29)

13   Patrick J. Wright, 'The Challenge of the Single Market', *CII Newsletter*, Vol.55, No.19, 17 December 1991, pp.1-3. See also *Ireland in Europe: A Shared Challenge – Economic Co-operation on the Island of Ireland in an Integrated Europe*, Dublin: Stationery Office, 1992.

14   See *Programme for Economic and Social Progress*, Dublin: Stationery Office, 1991, p.87.

15   For example, an informed conclusion as to what can be expected of multinational investment in the North reads: 'With rare exceptions the normal profile of larger inward investment projects locating in Northern Ireland is that of a branch plant or assembly operation lacking any real capacity to pursue an independent business strategy. In addition such projects are often among the smallest in capacity terms within their group and hence particularly vulnerable to closure when the market turns down or the parent company realigns its product mix. ...Inward investment has an important role to play in developing the economy but it is as an **adjunct** to the principal objective of promoting home industry and as **part of an integrated development process**' (Northern Ireland Economic Council, *Economic Strategy in Northern Ireland,* op. cit., n.6.45, p.67, emphasis added). See also Northern Ireland Economic Council, *Inward Investment in Northern Ireland,* Belfast: Northern Ireland Economic Development Office, 1992 (Report 99).

16   'Too few of our best students are drawn to a career in industry, much less to enterprise. Between 1971 and 1986 the number of accountants more than trebled, and the number of auctioneers and lawyers doubled, but the number of engineers increased by less than 50 per cent. While Ireland, like every society, needs its accountants and lawyers, it is hard to resist the conclusion that too little effort in Ireland is going into directly productive activities that are product-oriented and market-driven' (Industrial Policy Review Group, op. cit., p.22).

'It is not easy to explain such trends in occupational preferences in a country which needs to develop its industrial base and its export markets. Part of it can probably be explained in terms of the complexity of the tax code and other State regulations which increase the demand for professional advice of one kind or another. In general, it would appear that the rewards to ... (activity which redistributes existing assets ie."rent-seeking") can in many instances be far more attractive than those in productive activity' (The Central Bank, op. cit., para. 19, p.14).

'The "tax avoidance" industry which operates to use the system to the best advantage flourishes because of the flaws of the system and it would be unrealistic to expect business management of any enterprise to ignore it. ... tax anomalies divert resources and energy into areas which would not receive priority under criteria of business efficiency or cohesive policy' (Miriam Hederman O'Brien, 'The Role of Taxation in the Achievement of Social Justice', in Michael Reidy and Domhnall McCullough (eds.), *Principle and Profit: Corporate Responsibility in Ireland*, Dublin: Columba Press, 1992, pp.69-70).

17   For a discussion on the importance of the satisfactory socialisation of the means of production, see *Laborem Exercens*, n.14.

18 See *Northern Ireland Expenditure Plans and Priorities: The Government's Expenditure Plans 1992/93 - 1994/95*, London: HMSO, February 1992, p.155; T.J. Barrington, 'Local Government Reform: Problems to Resolve' in James A. Walsh (ed.), *Local Economic Development and Administrative Reform*, Dublin: Regional Studies Association (Irish Branch), 1991, Table 3, p.57; estimated expenditure data for the Republic (1992) from Department of the Environment, and Department of Finance, *Economic Review and Outlook 1992*, Dublin: Stationery Office, p.41.

19 The principle of subsidiarity, which has assumed prominence in debates within the European Community today, was implicit in Pope Leo XIII's discussion of the relative duties of the citizen and the State when he launched modern Church social teaching in 1891. However, it was Pope Pius XI who first formulated the principle succinctly in 1931 (see *Quadragesimo Anno (The Social Order)*, 15 May 1931, n.79). The importance of the principle is returned to in later documents of Church social teaching. (See Pope John XXIII, *Mater et Magistra (New Light on Social Problems)*, 15 May 1961, n.53; n.117, and *Gaudium et Spes (Pastoral Constitution on the Church in the Modern World)*, n.86 c.)

20 The Northern Ireland Economic Council has been unambiguous in this regard: 'The objectives which we have set out for economic strategy in the Province are ambitious. Achieving these objectives ... (implies) a very fundamental reappraisal of the relationship between the nature of policy making and implementation in the region and by central Government. For Northern Ireland to seek to grow much faster than the national economy ... means that the Province must have the freedom to order its affairs in ways which may differ fundamentally from the practice elsewhere in the UK' (Northern Ireland Economic Council, *Economic Strategy in Northern Ireland*, n.7.7, p.76).

International comparisons also suggest that thriving local democracy and good national economic performance may go hand-in-hand. For example, in Denmark whose GNP per person is very much higher than in Ireland '...a Danish person has more than twice the opportunity of being elected to Danish public service than a corresponding Irish person...' because their ratio of population to council seats is so much better. (See T.J. Barrington, 'The Future of Local Democracy', in Nuala Rearden (ed.), *Is There Local Democracy North or South?*, Proceedings of the Social Study Conference, August 1991, published by Social Study Conference, 1992.)

See also Michael J. Bannon, 'The Role of Local Government in Local Economic Development', in James A. Walsh (ed.), *Local Ecomonic Development and Administrative Reform,* op. cit.

21 'Regional policy pushed to the periphery many of the simpler, production-only plants that did not need to be close to head offices or to companies' principal factories. But it did not shift corporate headquarters, senior managerial teams or R and D establishments, which largely remained in the greater South East' (Stephen Fothergill and Nigel Guy, *Branch Factory Closures in Northern Ireland*, Belfast: Northern Ireland Economic Research Centre, 1990).

22 'The up-take and successful exploitation of all the new funds for rural development may be constrained by the endowment of entrepreneurial skills in rural areas in the short term. ... We all know how difficult it is to formulate local initiatives of an integrated nature. It is new territory for most communities now under tremendous pressure to readjust their activities and diversify the local economy and, despite the existence of the Operational Programme for Rural Development and the *LEADER* programme, many areas may not simply be in a position to provide matching

resources and acceptable programmes at the drop of a hat' (Brendan Kearney, 'Impact of Current Policies and Structures', Paper to 'Developing the West Together', Seminar sponsored by the Bishops of the West of Ireland, Galway, 4-5 November 1991).

'It is difficult for people whose principal sources of income for generations have been tied to... (mainstream agricultural activities) to fully comprehend that the future requires diversification and flexibility in the light of a wider understanding of just what the resources and opportunities facing them are' (The Council for Social Welfare, *Unemployment, Jobs and the 1990s*, op. cit., para.74, p.34).

23 Examples include where housing authorities have given unemployed local people part-time or full-time jobs in wholly new measures to protect and improve the quality of their homes and physical environment, or where health authorities could appreciate a local home-help service as a source of valuable employment and not merely as a cost-effective method of delivering community care.

24 See the Business in the Community organisation in the UK. The involvement of the private sector in the area-based response to long-term unemployment in the Republic's Programme for Economic and Social Progress (1991) is a welcome development. We hope that it, with its associated Enterprise Trust, will prove to have been a new stage in the development of corporate social responsibility in Ireland.

25 For an expert view on the importance of the European context to Northern Ireland see Northern Ireland Economic Council, *Northern Ireland: A Decade for Decision*, by Dr George Quigley, Annual Sir Charles Carter Lecture, 25 February 1992, Belfast: Northern Ireland Economic Develop-

ment Office, 1992 (Report 95). In that address business enterprise and the need for consensus in the management of Northern Ireland's economic affairs are also dealt with.

26 The words of the European Bishops are addressed to this island too:
'On the threshold of the third millennium, Europe is living through extraordinary events through which the loving and merciful hand of God the Father stretched out to all humanity, his children, is almost tangible. ... For Christians, these events demonstrate a genuine *kairos* in the history of salvation and they offer an immense challenge to carry on God's renewing work, on which the fate of the nations ultimately depends' (Special Assembly for Europe of the Synod of Bishops, 1991, Final Declaration, 'To Be Witnesses of Christ Who Has Set Us Free', *Catholic International*, Vol. 3, No. 5, 1-14 March 1992, pp.211-212).

27 See National Economic and Social Council, *A Strategy for the Nineties: Economic Stability and Structural Change,* op. cit., Table 6.5, p.171.

28 See The Council for Social Welfare, *Emerging Trends in the Social Welfare System?*, Dublin: The Council for Social Welfare, 1992, pp.2-5.

29 *Our View at Last, The Oval Report,* Dublin: Tallaght Centre for the Unemployed, 1992.

30 Research involving fourteen representative groups from disadvantaged areas of Belfast revealed that in relation to training schemes and allied initiatives, there was '...considerable dissatisfaction, irritation and exasperation.' Prominent among the concerns expressed were '...that schemes generally were **a poor substitute for more traditional methods** of training...'; the demoralising effect of poor quality

schemes; and that schemes were '**irrelevant** ... a device to reduce the unemployment statistics...' – the real need being for jobs. The writers of the report recalled the words of an earlier researcher: "'Each door they open leads to nowhere. These projects are continually adding anterooms which disguise the ultimate frustration'" (Northern Ireland Voluntary Trust, op. cit., Part I, p.25).

31 Their incentive, clearly, is the high marginal tax rate they face. Many unemployed people, however, find themselves living in deprived urban areas, where there is little money in circulation, and without the contacts, access to tools and transport that doing regular odd jobs requires. (See The Council for Social Welfare, *Unemployment, Jobs and the 1990s*, op. cit., para.114, p.50.)

32 Six years after the publication of the Report of the government-appointed Commission on Social Welfare, which examined, *inter alia*, the adequacy of social welfare payments, only 18 per cent of social welfare recipients in the Republic had weekly payments that met the recommended minimum, and those receiving unemployment compensation were not among them. (See Jo Murphy-Lawless, *The Adequacy of Income and Family Expenditure*, op. cit., p. xii.)

33 For a thorough analysis of the interaction between low pay on the one hand, and the social welfare and taxation systems on the other, in the South, see John Blackwell, 'Family Income Support: Policy Options', in Brigid Reynolds SM and Sean J Healy SMA (eds.), *Poverty and Family Income Policy*, Papers of a Social Policy Conference, Dublin, 30 September 1988, Dublin: Conference of Major Religious Superiors (Ireland), 1988, and National Economic and Social Council, *A Strategy for the Nineties: Economic Stability and Structural Change*, op. cit., pp.208-226.

34 For a comprehensive analysis of the evolution of part-time working in Northern Ireland see Northern Ireland Economic Council, *Part-Time Employment in Northern Ireland*, Belfast: Northern Ireland Ecomonic Development Office, October 1992 (Report 98).

PART FOUR

The Spirituality: A Spirituality for the Challenge

135. The task of witnessing to the dignity of human work, and of living out the virtue of solidarity in the face of unemployment and emigration, is one for the whole Church and for each member. Different people have different parts to play according to the variety of gifts which they have received (cf.1 Cor 12:4-11).

136. We bishops, through this Pastoral, seek to make a specific contribution as teachers to the resolution of unemployment and emigration. The contribution of the whole Church – that is, of the People of God – with numerous members in every sphere and walk of life throughout this island, has, however, to go far beyond words! It has to have a discernible economic, social and political impact. 'Bishops, clergy, religious and lay people are all ... called ... no-one has the right to stay idle.'[1] In the translation into **doing** of what we discuss in this Pastoral, we encourage the lay faithful to take the lead:

> '...it belongs to (them), without waiting passively for orders and directives, to take the initiative freely and to infuse a Christian spirit into the mentality, customs, laws and structures of the community in which they live. Changes are necessary, basic reforms are indispensable; lay people should strive resolutely to permeate them with the spirit of the Gospel' (*Populorum Progressio*, n.81).

137. This will not be easy. Reducing unemployment in Ireland is a daunting task, but it is not impossible. What makes it difficult is that every one of us, every group, every agency, is being called to some change. If our society has not been torn apart by the high unemployment of today, it is because the majority of us are quite comfortable. It is easier to identify the changes others should make than those we ourselves should make; it is easy to point to what others are failing to do while justifying our own failure to act.

138. The fundamental starting point in this task is the heart and the mind of the individual person:
'This difficult road of the indispensable transformation of the structures of economic life is one on which it will not be easy to go forward without the intervention of a true conversion of mind, will and heart' (*Redemptor Hominis*, n.16).

139. The first appeal we make, therefore, to each and every person is this: in order to be part of the solution rather than part of the problem, look to Christ! Allow Christ to '...walk with ... (you) the path of life, with the power of the truth about ... (the human person) and the world that is contained in the mystery of the Incarnation and Redemption and with the power of the love that is radiated by that truth' (*Redemptor Hominis*, n.39).

140. People who open their hearts and minds to Christ, to that intimate Companion who walks with them the road of their life, find a purpose in life, deeper and more durable than that which any job can give, a purpose so powerful that they become capable of witnessing to the dignity of human work no matter what job they hold and even when they are unemployed.

141. In our listening we were privileged to glimpse this reality in the lives of different people. Vast as the scale of the problem is, we are aware that the Church is present in boardroom and dole queue. Everywhere, baptised and confirmed men and women, filled with the gifts of the Holy Spirit and believing the message of the Gospel, are present and are anxious to find ways of witnessing to the dignity of human work and of practising the virtue of solidarity.

142. In their daily lives, this witness and this practice can give occasion for real participation in the **passover** of the Lord. That is to say, the individual can experience just what it is to die to self and live to others in the power of the Spirit which Jesus gives. Two ways in which very many people experience this are in holding fast to the integrity of their work, and in insisting on showing respect for public money.

(i) The Spirituality of Work

143. The danger is alive today, in every employment and profession, of choosing what one does, and valuing it, solely by the amount of money it brings in. One's work, one's skills, knowledge and experience, are seen primarily as a lever for extracting purchasing power. In such a climate, it takes moral courage to decide that one's work is primarily about people, relating to and serving other people while becoming more of a human being in the process. Of course a job must bring in a fair wage, but the purpose of life is not just to earn but to serve, and, to Christians, their jobs are a vitally important means of serving others. They know that their work has a value in itself, because it is **their** work, because it is expressing their love for others and their appreciation of creation with their own small part in it.

144. This approach by people to their work means that they are standing on a rock (Mt 7:24-25). Such people will not be blindly led by what everyone else appears to be doing[2] but, in and through their places of work, will be capable of questioning, for example, the claims their own group is making on public revenue or the availability of systematic overtime to them.

(ii) Respect for What is Public

145. No matter what the political complexion of the government of the day, our modern industrial societies are complex organisms in which the co-operation and mutual responsibility of millions of people are exercised through the fiscal (taxation and public expenditure) activities of public authorities. The Christian will be the first to feel indignant at examples of public inefficiency or distorted priorities. However, she or he will be the last to use disappointment or disgust with public figures or public policies to justify a lowering of personal standards in payment of taxes or use of public funds. It is pure rationalisation and a selfish undermining of the common good to think that it is legitimate to have taken this

money, or not to pay it, because 'I am going to use it more responsibly than the government would.' Christians are capable of seeing in all public money the income of their brothers and sisters who are unemployed, the grant that will keep a community group in existence, the investment that will provide jobs for others.

146. Ambiguity towards the payment of tax or one's right to a public payment is particularly damaging in the Republic. The large number of its youth who have emigrated, the high unemployment at home, and the – partially induced – low participation rate of women in paid employment combine to give it an extraordinarily high dependency ratio.[3] When the piecemeal development of its taxation system, with the granting of breaks and reliefs to many special interest groups and the consequent narrowing of the tax base, is added to this, it is clear what moral integrity and courage is required in the Republic today to respect public money to the full.

(iii) The Advance of the Kingdom of God

147. The witness that Christians have to give in the world of work today extends beyond the integrity with which they undertake their own work and their honesty with the State.

> 'In the context of the transformations taking place in the world of economy and work which are a cause of concern, the lay faithful have the responsibility of being in the forefront in working out a solution to the very serious problems of growing unemployment; to fight for the most opportune overcoming of numerous injustices that come from organisations of work which lack a proper goal; to make the workplace become a community of persons respected in their uniqueness and in their right to participation; to develop new solidarity among those that participate in a common work; to raise up new forms of entrepreneurship and to look again at systems of commerce, finance and exchange of technology' (*Christifideles Laici*, n.43).[4]

148. Such formidable challenges can make our efforts seem puny and ineffectual. The revelation of God's love in Christ comes to transform that sense of helplessness. We recognise that the world is in God's hands and that, in divine Providence, no work for justice, no act of solidarity, is ever wasted. It is a welcoming of the new creation of justice, love and peace which is already established in the Resurrection. Christ assures those who trust in the love of God that '...the way of love lies open to all... and that the effort to establish a universal human solidarity will not be in vain' (*Gaudium et Spes*, n.38).

149. In the light of faith, the human virtue of solidarity[5] is immensely deepened. The unity of the human race, which is founded on the reality of God, **their** love and divine mercy, cannot remain simply in the area of giving people their rights. It must be ready to give what can never be demanded as a right – forgiveness and love:

> 'Beyond human and natural bonds, already so close and so strong, there is discerned in the light of faith a new *model* of the *unity* of the human race, which must ultimately inspire our *solidarity*. This supreme *model of unity*, which is a reflection of the intimate life of God, one God in three Persons, is what we Christians mean by the word "communion"' (*Sollicitudo Rei Socialis*, n.40).

150. Jesus frequently spoke about the Kingdom or state of affairs which **His Father** was intent on establishing. While making its demands on us, this Kingdom is nevertheless a gift (Lk 12:32). There every human being is offered a welcome, every human gift its unimaginable flourishing, every human relationship its eternal fulfilment. As Christians we are called to place all our efforts to see the dignity of each person's work in the context of this building of the Kingdom.

151. This realisation that God is building the Kingdom of peace **through us** gives us that peculiar Christian balance of serenity

and urgency. Despite the resistance we experience, in ourselves as well as in others, we do not give in. Despite the apparent smallness of the results, we do not give up. Our one shame would be to not play our part.

> 'Far from diminishing our concern to develop this earth, the expectancy of a new earth should spur us on, for it is here that the body of a new human family grows, foreshadowing in some way the age which is to come. That is why, although we must be careful to distinguish earthly progress from the increase of the kingdom of Christ, such progress is of vital concern to the kingdom of God, insofar as it can contribute to the better ordering of human society. ... Here on earth the kingdom is mysteriously present; when the Lord comes it will enter into its perfection' (*Gaudium et Spes*, n.39).[6]

✠ CAHAL CARDINAL DALY
Archbishop of Armagh

✠ DESMOND CONNELL
Archbishop of Dublin

✠ JOSEPH CASSIDY
Archbishop of Tuam

✠ DERMOT CLIFFORD
Archbishop of Cashel

REFERENCES

1   The Grail, *This is the Laity: Simplification of 'Christifideles Laic*i', London: The Grail, 1989, n.2, p.9; n.3, p.11.

      See also:
      Irish Commission for the Laity, *Topics on the Laity from the Apostolic Exhortation of Pope John Paul II*, Dublin: Irish Commission for the Laity, 1989;

      Irish Commission for the Laity, *Study Guide on 'Christifideles Laici'*, Dublin: Irish Commission for the Laity, 1990.

2   *The Work of Justice: Irish Bishops' Pastoral*, op. cit., paras. 60-61, pp.28-29.

3   See reference 7, Part Three, p.77.

4   Pope John Paul II, *Christifideles Laici (The Vocation and Mission of the Lay Faithful in the Church and in the World)*, 30 December 1988, Dublin: Veritas Publications.

5   See paragraphs 75-80.

6   Vatican II, *Gaudium et Spes (Pastoral Constitution on the Church in the Modern World)*, 7 December 1965, in Austin Flannery OP (General Editor), *Vatican II: The Conciliar and Post-Conciliar Documents* (revised edition), Collegeville, MN: Liturgical Press, 1984.

BIBLIOGRAPHY

I CHURCH SOCIAL TEACHING

(i) Papal and Vatican Documents

POPE LEO XIII, *Rerum Novarum (On the Condition of Workers)*, 15 May 1891, London: Catholic Truth Society.

POPE PIUS XI, *Quadragesimo Anno (The Social Order)*, 15 May 1931, London: Catholic Truth Society.

POPE JOHN XXIII, *Mater et Magistra (New Light on Social Problems)*, 15 May 1961, London: Catholic Truth Society.

POPE JOHN XXIII, *Pacem in Terris (Peace on Earth)*, 11 April 1963, London: Catholic Truth Society.

VATICAN II, *Gaudium et Spes (Pastoral Constitution on the Church in the Modern World)*, 7 December 1965, London: Catholic Truth Society.

POPE PAUL VI, *Populorum Progressio (The Development of Peoples)*, 26 March 1967, London: Catholic Truth Society.

POPE PAUL VI, *Octogesima Adveniens (The Eightieth Anniversary)*, 15 May 1971, London: Catholic Truth Society.

POPE PAUL VI, *Evangelii Nuntiandi (Evangelization in the Modern World)*, 8 December 1975, London: Catholic Truth Society.

POPE JOHN PAUL II, *Redemptor Hominis (Redeemer of Man)*, 4 March 1979, London: Catholic Truth Society.

POPE JOHN PAUL II, *Laborem Exercens (On Human Work)*, 14 September 1981, London: Catholic Truth Society.

CONGREGATION FOR THE DOCTRINE OF THE FAITH, *Libertatis Nuntius (Instruction on Certain Aspects of the 'Theology of Liberation')*, 6 August 1984, London: Catholic Truth Society.

CONGREGATION FOR THE DOCTRINE OF THE FAITH, *Libertatis Conscientia (Instruction on Christian Freedom and Liberation)*, 22 March 1986, London: Catholic Truth Society.

POPE JOHN PAUL II, *Sollicitudo Rei Socialis (The Social Concern of the Church)*, 30 December 1987, London: Catholic Truth Society.

POPE JOHN PAUL II, *Christifideles Laici (The Vocation and Mission of the Lay Faithful in the Church and in the World)*, 30 December 1988, Dublin: Veritas Publications.

POPE JOHN PAUL II, *Centesimus Annus (The Hundredth Anniversary)*, 1 May 1991, London: Catholic Truth Society.

(ii)   Other Texts; Commentaries

ABBOTT, WALTER M, SJ (General Editor), *The Documents of Vatican II*, London: Geoffrey Chapman, 1966.

BAUM, GREGORY, *The Priority of Labor: A Commentary on Laborem Exercens, Encyclical Letter of Pope John Paul II*, New York/Ramsey: Paulist Press, 1982.

CALVEZ, JEAN-YVES, and PERRIN, JACQUES, *The Church and Social Justice: The Social Teaching of the Popes from Leo XIII to Pius XII, 1878-1958*, Chicago: Regnery, 1961.

CARRIER, HERVÉ SJ, *The Social Doctrine of the Church Revisited: A Guide for Study*, Vatican City: Pontifical Council for Justice and Peace, 1990.

Christian Faith in a Time of Economic Depression, A Statement from the Irish Episcopal Conference at its General Meeting, 15 June 1983.

Christians and the Ecological Crisis, Pope John Paul II's Message for 1990 World Day of Peace on the Theme 'Peace with God the Creator, Peace with All Creation', Dublin: Irish Commission for Justice and Peace.

The Church in the Present-Day Transformation of Latin America in the Light of the Council, Conclusions of the Second General Conference of the Latin American Bishops, Medellin, 24 August - 6 September 1968, second edition, Washington DC: United States Catholic Conference, Division for Latin America, 1973.

DORR, DONAL, *Option for the Poor: A Hundred Years of Vatican Social Teaching*, Dublin: Gill & Macmillan, 1983.

Emigration: A Pastoral Letter from the Bishops of the West of Ireland, Sunday 15 March 1987.

FLANNERY, AUSTIN, OP (General Editor), *Vatican II: The Conciliar and Post Conciliar Documents* (revised edition), Collegeville, MN: Liturgical Press, 1984.

THE GRAIL, *This is the Laity: Simplification of 'Christifideles Laici'*, London: The Grail, 1989.

GREMILLION, JOSEPH (ed.), *The Gospel of Peace and Justice: Catholic Social Teaching Since Pope John*, Maryknoll: Orbis, 1976.

IRISH COMMISSION FOR THE LAITY, *Study Guide on 'Christifideles Laici'*, Dublin: Irish Commission for the Laity, 1990.

IRISH COMMISSION FOR THE LAITY, *Topics on the Laity from the Apostolic Exhortation of Pope John Paul II*, Dublin: Irish Commission for the Laity, 1989.

John Paul II in Mexico: His Collected Speeches, London: Collins, 1979.

Justice in the World, Document of The Second General Assembly of the Synod of Bishops, November 1971, Vatican City: Vatican Polyglot Press.

MOLONY, JOHN, *The Worker Question - A New Historical Perspective on Rerum Novarum*, Dublin: Gill & Macmillan, 1991.

PONTIFICAL COMMISSION FOR JUSTICE AND PEACE, *At the Service of the Human Community: An Ethical Approach to the International Debt Question,* 27 December 1986, London: Catholic Truth Society.

PONTIFICAL COMMISSION FOR JUSTICE AND PEACE, *What Have You Done to Your Homeless Brother? The Church and the Housing Problem,* Document of the Pontifical Commission on the Occasion of the International Year of Shelter for the Homeless, 27 December 1987, Dublin: Veritas Publications.

PONTIFICAL COUNCIL FOR JUSTICE AND PEACE, *Human Rights and the Church: Historical and Theological Reflections*, Conferences Presented at an International Colloquium, Rome, 14-16 November 1988, Vatican City: Pontifical Council for Justice and Peace, 1990.

PONTIFICAL COUNCIL FOR JUSTICE AND PEACE, *Social and Ethical Aspects of Economics*, A Colloquium in the Vatican, Vatican City: Pontifical Council for Justice and Peace, 1992.

The Pope in Ireland: Addresses and Homilies, Dublin: Veritas Publications, 1979.

Puebla: Evangelization at Present and in the Future of Latin America, Conclusions of the Third General Conference of Latin American Bishops, 27 January - 13 February 1979, Official English Edition, Slough: St Paul Publications/London: Catholic Institute for International Relations, 1980.

US NATIONAL CONFERENCE OF CATHOLIC BISHOPS, *Economic Justice for All: Pastoral Letter on Catholic Social Teaching and the US Economy*, Washington DC: United States Catholic Conference, 1986.

Ways of Peace: Papal Messages for the World Days of Peace, Vatican City: Pontifical Council for Justice and Peace, 1986.

The Work of Justice: Irish Bishops' Pastoral, Dublin: Veritas Publications, 1977.

II   ECONOMIC AND SOCIAL SOURCES CITED

BANNON, MICHAEL J., 'The Role of Local Government in Local Economic Development', in James A. Walsh (ed.), *Local Economic Development and Administrative Reform*, Dublin: Regional Studies Association (Irish Branch), 1991.

BARRINGTON, T.J., 'Local Government Reform: Problems to Resolve', in James A. Walsh (ed.), op. cit.

BARRINGTON, T.J., 'The Future of Local Democracy', in Nuala Rearden (ed.), *Is There Local Democracy North or South?*, Proceedings of the Social Study Conference, 1991, published by Social Study Conference, 1992.

BLACKWELL, JOHN, 'Family Income Support: Policy Options', in Brigid Reynolds SM and Sean J. Healy SMA (eds.), *Poverty and Family Income Policy*, Papers of a Social Policy Conference, Dublin, 30 September 1988, Dublin: Conference of Major Religious Superiors (Ireland), 1988.

CALLAN, T., NOLAN, B. and WHELAN, B.J., HANNAN D.F., with CREIGHTON, S., *Poverty, Income and Welfare in Ireland*, Dublin: The Economic and Social Research Institute, 1989 (General Research Series, Paper No.146).

CATHOLIC SOCIAL SERVICE CONFERENCE, *Dublin: Hard Facts, Future Hopes*, Dublin: Catholic Social Service Conference, 1988.

THE CENTRAL BANK, *Submission on Industrial Policy: A Report to the Industrial Policy Review Group*, Dublin: Stationery Office, 1992.

COMBAT POVERTY AGENCY, *Pictures of Poverty: Twelve Accounts of Life on Low Income*, Dublin: Combat Poverty Agency, 1989.

THE COUNCIL FOR SOCIAL WELFARE, *Emerging Trends in the Social Welfare System?*, Dublin: The Council for Social Welfare, 1992.

THE COUNCIL FOR SOCIAL WELFARE, *Unemployment, Jobs and the 1990s*, Dublin: The Council for Social Welfare, 1989.

DOUTHWAITE, RICHARD, *The Growth Illusion*, Dublin: Lilliput Press, 1992.

EMIGRANT ADVICE, *Annual Report 1991*, Dublin: Emigrant Advice.

EVASON, EILEEN, *On the Edge: A Study of Poverty and Long-term Unemployment in Northern Ireland*, London: Child Poverty Action Group, 1985 (Poverty Pamphlet 69).

EVASON, EILEEN, ALLAMBY, LES and WOODS, ROBERTA, *The Deserving and the Undeserving Poor – The Social Fund in Northern Ireland*, Derry: Child Poverty Action Group (Northern Ireland), 1990.

FINNEGAN, BISHOP THOMAS A., 'Developing the West Together', *The Furrow*, Vol.43, No.4, April 1992.

FORSYTHE, FRANK P. and BOROOAH, VANI K., 'The Nature of Migration Between Northern Ireland and Great Britain: A Preliminary Analysis Based on the Labour Force Surveys, 1986-88', *The Economic and Social Review*, Vol. 23, No.2, January 1992.

FOTHERGILL, STEPHEN and GUY, NIGEL, *Branch Factory Closures in Northern Ireland:* Belfast, Northern Ireland Economic Research Centre, 1990.

GREENSLADE, LIAM, 'White Skins: White Masks, Psychological Distress Amongst the Irish in Britain', in Patrick O'Sullivan (ed.), *The Irish in the New Communities*, Leicester: Leicester University Press, 1992.

GREENSLADE, LIAM, PEARSON, MAGGIE and MADDEN, MOSS, *Irish Migrants in Britain: Socio-Economic and Demographic Conditions*, Liverpool: Institute of Irish Studies, University of Liverpool, 1991 (Occasional Papers in Irish Studies, No.3).

HANNAN, D.F. and SHORTHALL, S., *The Quality of Their Education: School Leavers' Views of Educational Objectives and Outcomes,* Dublin: The Economic and Social Research Institute, 1991 (General Research Series, Paper No.153).

HEALY, JOHN, *Nineteen Acres*, Achill: The House of Healy, 1987 (first published by Kenny's Bookshop, Galway, 1978).

HEALY, JOHN, *No One Shouted Stop*, Achill: The House of Healy, 1988 (first published as *The Death of An Irish Town*, by Mericer Press, Cork, 1968).

HEDERMAN-O'BRIEN, MIRIAM, 'The Role of Taxation in the Achievement of Social Justice', in Michael Reidy and Domhnall

McCullough (eds.), *Principle and Profit: Corporate Responsibility in Ireland*, Dublin: Columba Press, 1992.

INDUSTRIAL POLICY REVIEW GROUP, *A Time for Change: Industrial Policy for the 1990s* (The Culliton Report), Dublin: Stationery Office, 1992.

The Information Needs of Emigrants, Report of a Seminar Jointly Organised by The Action Group for Irish Youth (London), Emigrant Advice Unit (Belfast), Emigrant Advice (Dublin) and The National Youth Council of Ireland, Dublin, 9 December 1991.

Ireland in Europe: A Shared Challenge – Economic Co-operation on the Island of Ireland in an Integrated Europe, Dublin: Stationery Office, 1992.

THE IRISH EPISCOPAL COMMISSION FOR EMIGRANTS, *Emigrant Survey 1991/1992*, Dublin: The Irish Episcopal Commission for Emigrants, 1992.

THE IRISH EPISCOPAL COMMISSION FOR EMIGRANTS and THE CATECHETICAL ASSOCIATION OF IRELAND, *Far Away Hills: Christian Perspectives on Emigration*, A Manual for Teachers and Group Leaders, Dublin: The Irish Episcopal Commission for Emigrants, 1990.

KENNEDY, K.A., GIBLIN, T. and McHUGH, D., *The Economic Development of Ireland in the Twentieth Century*, London and New York: Routledge, 1988.

LEE, PAULINE and GIBNEY, MICHAEL, *Patterns of Food and Nutrient Intake in a Suburb of Dublin with Chronically High Unemployment*, Dublin: Combat Poverty Agency, 1988.

LEE, J.J., 'Society and Culture', in Frank Litton (ed.), *Unequal Achievement: The Irish Experience 1957-1982*, Dublin: Institute of Public Administration, 1982.

LEE, J.J., *Politics and Society: Ireland, 1912-1985*, Cambridge: Cambridge University Press, 1989.

MURPHY-LAWLESS, JO, *The Adequacy of Income and Family Expenditure*, Dublin: Combat Poverty Agency, 1992.

NATIONAL ECONOMIC AND SOCIAL COUNCIL, *A Strategy for the Nineties: Economic Stability and Structural Change*, Dublin: National Economic and Social Council, 1990 (Report No.89).

NATIONAL ECONOMIC AND SOCIAL COUNCIL, *Ireland in the European Community: Performance, Prospects and Strategy*, Dublin: National Economic and Social Council, 1989 (Report No.88).

NATIONAL ECONOMIC AND SOCIAL COUNCIL, *The Economic and Social Implications of Emigration*, Dublin: National Economic and Social Council, 1991 (Report No.90).

NOLAN, BRIAN and FARRELL, BRIAN, *Child Poverty in Ireland*, Dublin: Combat Poverty Agency, 1990.

NORTHERN IRELAND ECONOMIC COUNCIL, *Economic Strategy in Northern Ireland*, Belfast: Northern Ireland Economic Development Office, 1991 (Report 88).

NORTHERN IRELAND ECONOMIC COUNCIL, *The Food Processing Industry in Northern Ireland*, Belfast: Northern Ireland Economic Development Office, 1992 (Report 92).

NORTHERN IRELAND ECONOMIC COUNCIL, *Inward Investment in Northern Ireland*, Belfast: Northern Ireland Economic Development Office, 1992 (Report 99).

NORTHERN IRELAND ECONOMIC COUNCIL, *Northern Ireland: A Decade for Decision*, by Dr George Quigley, Annual Sir Charles

Carter Lecture, 25 February 1992, Belfast: Northern Ireland Economic Development Office, 1992 (Report 95).

NORTHERN IRELAND ECONOMIC COUNCIL, *Part-time Employment in Northern Ireland*, Belfast: Northern Ireland Economic Development Office, 1992 (Report 98).

NORTHERN IRELAND VOLUNTARY TRUST, *A Qualitative Study of Life in the Disadvantaged Areas of Belfast*, Belfast: Northern Ireland Voluntary Trust, 1991.

OECD, *Employment Outlook*, July 1991, Paris: Organisation for Economic Co-operation and Development.

Our View At Last: The Oval Report, Dublin: Tallaght Centre for the Unemployed, 1992.

OPPENHEIM, CAREY, *Poverty: The Facts*, London: Child Poverty Action Group, 1990.

PEARSON, MAGGIE, MADDEN, MOSS and GREENSLADE, LIAM, *Generations of an Invisible Minority: The Health and Well Being of the Irish in Britain*, Liverpool: Institute of Irish Studies, University of Liverpool, 1992 (Occasional Papers in Irish Studies, No.2).

Programme for Economic and Social Progress, Dublin: Stationery Office, 1991.

RANDALL, GEOFFREY, *Over Here: Young Irish Migrants in London*, London: Action Group for Irish Youth, 1991.

THE REVENUE COMMISSIONERS, *Annual Report 1991*, Dublin: Stationery Office, July 1992.

TALLAGHT CENTRE FOR THE UNEMPLOYED, *Life on the Dole*, Dublin: Tallaght Centre for the Unemployed, 1991.

WHELAN, CHRISTOPHER T. and HANNAN, DAMIAN F., CREIGHTON, SEAN, *Unemployment, Poverty and Psychological Distress*, Dublin: The Economic and Social Research Institute, 1991 (General Research Series, Paper No.150).

WRIGHT, PATRICK J., 'The Challenge of the Single Market', *CII Newsletter*, Vol.55, No.19, 17 December 1991.